Conran +
Partners

For Terence Conran

First published in 2020 by Lund Humphries

Lund Humphries
Office 3, Book House
261A City Road
London EC1V 1JX
UK

www.lundhumphries.com

ISBN: 978-1-84822-343-1
A Cataloguing-in-Publication record for this book is available
from the British Library

Copy edited by Julie Gunz
Designed by Zoë Bather
Set in Platform and Lyon
Printed in Slovenia

Dominic Bradbury

Conran + Partners
A Way of Living

LUND
HUMPHRIES

Design is the legacy of thought; consequently thought is the legacy of design.

As designers, we are mindful that, in essence, we are engineering the experiences and perceptions of those who interact with our designs. Often, designing buildings can seem like one of the ultimate challenges to creativity as there are so many complex and interdependent issues for a designer to consider whilst undertaking a project. The overarching objective is always to create a timeless quality of place that will be enjoyed and appreciated long into the future, without becoming tired or unfashionable.

While there are many varied factors to consider in this process, such as interpersonal skills, engineering integrity, cost and aesthetics, it is the people – whether visitors or inhabitants – that are the ultimate judges of our success. Architecture may well be a commercial activity, but it is also one that needs to engender lasting appeal that satisfies not just the developer and planner, but also enhances the quality of life of a visitor, occupier or local community for many years.

Whether architecture or interior design, new-build or repurposing and refurbishing an existing site, it is vital that the project and process is as well planned as the detailed design and fabrication of the building itself. The Conran and Partners' ethos is to create not just good, but outstanding design solutions, which can be considered as the sum of insight, imaginative thought and vision, combined with skill and experience.

Conran and Partners has a rare breadth of experience working across a range of markets throughout the world, from elegant boutique interiors to major buildings and significant master planning projects. The partners all share a passion for creating thoughtful and elegant solutions that are uplifting to experience and inhabit. Their belief is that one must thoroughly understand the brief in its context – human, cultural and physical – before even putting pencil to paper.

Ultimately, close collaboration is the key to the success of Conran and Partners. The team appreciates that intelligence and ideas are often created and nurtured through rigorous discussion – not only with clients and consultants, but also with planners and local communities, all of whom can positively influence a narrative of the future design vision.

Sebastian Conran studied Industrial Design Engineering and has spent his career designing world-class innovative products, initially overseeing Habitat Mothercare's non-textile design studio, then founding Sebastian Conran Associates and later as Director responsible for product and graphic design at Conran and Partners. He is a founding trustee of the Design Museum and also has strong links with higher education as Designer in Residence at University of Sheffield, visiting Professor at Bristol Robotics Lab, past visiting Professor at Central Saint Martins and lecturer at the Royal College of Art. A leading design advocate, he speaks and lectures frequently, often focusing on the emotional engagement of design and the transformation of academic engineering research into satisfying consumer experiences. As a world-class designer he has written several books and papers on design and has received many academic honours, international industry awards and patents for his design and innovation work.

< An urban retreat in the sky with panoramic views, Boundary, London

Conran and Partners has a portfolio that extends around the world and embraces a rich and varied range of projects. As a collective, the six partners have a wide-ranging global frame of reference, yet their work is always rooted in specific local contexts. This fusion of international and local is held together by a design philosophy that places a particular importance upon narrative threads, giving all projects – wherever they are – a highly distinctive character.

The history of Conran and Partners stretches back to the early 1980s. The practice began life in London as a multidisciplinary firm (originally known as Conran Roche) founded by Sir Terence Conran and Fred Roche. As well as restaurants, early work included highly ambitious and innovative projects such as the master planning and phased design of Butler's Wharf (see page 142). Spanning a decade, this project included the original Design Museum building, as well as the creation of many new homes above now iconic riverside restaurants, all in a previously redundant but key London site. A number of other early commissions also related to Terence's game-changing interventions in the British retail and restaurant industries, through the Habitat stores, The Conran Shop and numerous Conran restaurants.

The practice has subsequently built up more than three decades of international experience in a wide variety of environments. In each case, the rigorous design process adopted by the whole team involves an immersive research process that seeks to establish a clear and full understanding of the historical, architectural, social and cultural context in which they are working, as well as the aspirations of the future occupants of their buildings.

Whilst most of the partners are trained architects, Conran and Partners' expertise spans many different aspects of design and covers architecture, interior design and master planning. Nonetheless, the practice's carefully considered design approach – from the micro to the macro, from inside to outside and back again – is founded upon an overriding belief in the power of understanding the context of the project and placing the users' needs at the forefront of all thought processes. The practice is well placed to see the bigger picture, with a constant overlap and interplay between architecture, interiors and place-making, and the partners' experience across a range of scales, encompassing everything from urban planning to fine detailing.

<1. **1.** A key way-finder in Central London, Centre Point Tower, London **2.** The collector's lounge, KEF Music Gallery, Hong Kong **3.** Conran and Partners' London studio

2.

This considered design philosophy provides the bond that holds together a collective of six partners focusing on architecture and interiors – Tim Bowder-Ridger, Lee Davies, Simon Kincaid, Tina Norden and Victoria Whenray, with Hardip Nijjar managing the financial governance of the practice. Each partner has particular areas of expertise and knowledge which enable them to assume leadership roles for projects that suit their specific strengths. These range from large-scale housing regeneration projects to individual restaurants and boutiques, from luxury hotels to the restoration and reinvention of mid-century buildings. The practice is known for its complementary areas of expertise, resulting in a dynamic and agile working environment.

The blurring of boundaries between disciplines adds something valuable to each project, as ideas are allowed to flow between one discipline to another. The practice's reinvention of Centre Point Tower in central London (see page 33) is a prime example of this, where an appreciation of the bigger picture has been critical to fusing place-making, architecture and interior design, while drawing inspiration from the location, the mid-century history of the building itself and the extraordinary opportunity it provides to residents.

A focus on character and personality sits at the heart of all of Conran and Partners' projects. With the reinvention of heritage buildings, there may be a strong contextual foundation already in place that needs to be protected, revealed and enhanced within the design process. At other times, the personality of a new-build project has to be established from scratch, drawing upon the wider context of the surroundings and the cultural framework of the location. For instance, the practice has been working on two new interior design projects for Park Hyatt in Jakarta and Auckland. Whilst they might have similar functions, they are very different in character because they are rooted in two strikingly different and vibrant contexts. This contextual approach must be balanced by considering how buildings and spaces are used and felt by their users. Empathy is therefore a very important word for the practice. Most of all, it recognises the importance of individuals and how each person using the building interacts on a daily basis with the space around them.

'Strong narratives, rooted in a sense of place, and the experiences of the project's end-users, inform our designs, enabling us to cross the boundaries between uses and different design disciplines to create a more rounded experience of modern living', says Principal, Tim Bowder-Ridger. 'That's where the richness in our work comes from. A key part of our job is communicating an idea and the only way that we can convey the complexity of what we do is by building strong and clear narratives for each project we work on. Storytelling is therefore an essential part of the design process. With restaurants and hotels, for instance, we create an experience that is four-dimensional – it's about space, food, service and behaviour. But we are now taking this way of thinking beyond hotels and restaurants and into residential, retail and working spaces. Our task is to create ways of living by considering how people really want to enjoy the experience of spaces, whether they are internal or external. It's about the whole journey that users make through those spaces and getting into the discipline of building narratives based on their emotional and practical needs.'

Conran and Partners offers a versatility that results in projects that are both cohesive and multifaceted, but always focused on the people experiencing the buildings or spaces. It is with this in mind that the practice rarely uses industry terms such as 'residential', 'hospitality' and 'master planning' to describe its work, but instead uses words such as 'home', 'pleasure' and 'place'.

'The different kinds of buildings and projects that the practice undertakes share far more similarities than differences', says Bowder-Ridger. 'Ultimately, buildings and the built environment are about creating a sensory experience, whether it's a door handle or a crafted façade, and about appreciating how different senses come into play in response to particular spaces. This means that even when working at a bigger scale, the practice can still focus on the smallest details. This is key because every detail in an architectural and design project has a purpose and must be coherent to the overall narrative approach to ensure the story remains tangible . . . not just to the designers but also to the users.'

Looking to the future, the notion of empathetic design remains a crucial concern within an outlook founded upon optimism and the practice's ability – as a collective of viewpoints – to engage with all kinds of design opportunities. In the real world, the disciplines of hospitality, residential and retail increasingly overlap, as entrepreneurs and developers look to create more immersive, experiential and multifaceted destination spaces. Conran and Partners is well placed to explore this hinterland.

Home

For Conran and Partners, home encapsulates many different residential typologies and contexts, as well as a range of scales and price points. In a world that is becoming ever more urbanised, considering how people can live and make their homes in cities in a way that enhances their quality of life has become one of the most critical concerns for our society. As a practice, Conran and Partners creates high-quality homes for people across the economic spectrum.

The practice brings a unique perspective to its design approach. As a team of architects, designers and master planners, they see the bigger picture, not just a small part of it. As such, Tim Bowder-Ridger explains, 'we focus on the spatial and volumetric quality of each element of a project as well as the sensual and tactile. Often we are commissioned to consider this for an entire building as architects and interior designers. At other times the practice is involved in collaborative schemes – with buildings designed by others. In this instance, a constant dialogue ensures an essential synergy between architecture and interiors, and between the public and private realms, as the journey progresses from outside to inside.'

Many projects recycle older structures, with all of their embodied energy, and help preserve and protect important examples of architectural heritage, while also giving them a fresh relevance.

'We now have an established track record in helping to breathe new life back into what may have become unloved buildings', says Bowder-Ridger. 'Whether for similar or different uses, our approach is to understand a building and its unique character. The research required often takes a bit of time and care but it's essential when you are dealing with such important buildings. It is this level of forensic understanding that distinguishes the work of the practice.'

Contrastingly, Conran and Partners is also involved in highly ambitious new residential developments and projects in cities as far apart as London and Tokyo. As with other project types, these are developed to reinforce a sense of context and character, as well as an empathy towards the resident, as demonstrated by Kita Aoyama in Tokyo (see page 42). The focus on empathy spans all of Conran and Partners' portfolio, yet has a particular significance when it comes to homes. The team attempts to understand the dreams, desires and daily needs of the residents and then works to manifest them in the design of the buildings.

1. Concept sketch, Portobello Square, London **2.** Cadence, London

3.

Within the apartments designed by the practice, the fusion of architectural and interior design skills results in an enhanced sense of space and light, as well as the natural flow from one area to another. There are also spatial skills and principles that cross-fertilise between the practice's work in the luxury marketplace and in social housing, where Conran and Partners has become very active over the last decade.

Increasingly, these are projects that draw inspiration from the world of hotel and hospitality design, incorporating vibrant lobbies and reception zones, communal spaces and amenities such as gyms, pools, libraries and screening rooms. Given its extensive expertise within the hospitality sector (see Pleasure, beginning on page 70), the practice is well placed to carry such ideas into residential concepts. 'One of the reasons that residential projects are becoming more intriguing is because the cross-over with the hospitality sector is moving closer and closer all the time', Bowder-Ridger explains.

'We are designing cinemas, lounges, work spaces and screening rooms within residential projects, all of which add value and identity to the project whilst making them feel more like hotels. Equally, our hotel clients are talking about bringing a residential atmosphere to their businesses. So, it's a cross-over that actually goes both ways for us and centres on an understanding of a contemporary experience.'

The practice's approach is informed by its experience in different disciplines and sectors, and in different parts of the world. More and more people are looking for a sense of place, individuality and personality. This drives the team to constantly challenge sometimes lazy industry assumptions of what quality homes might be, assumptions that too often rest simply on what has been done before and which tend to generate mediocre solutions.

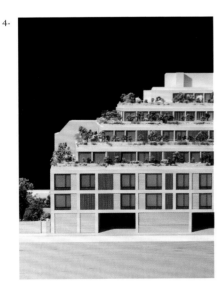

4.

3. Centre Point Tower, London 4. Architectural model, Kita Aoyama, Tokyo

Richard Rogers' and Renzo Piano's landmark Centre Pompidou in Paris was one building that made a particular impression on Victoria Whenray as a student. This Beaubourg landmark is one of the great examples of high-tech architecture. Equally important to her was the open piazza, included as part of the original competition entry, which complements this internationally renowned museum of modern art. Whenray recalls, 'it was just before I started studying architecture when I first visited the museum with some friends. We emerged from inside just minutes after the end of a particularly heavy rainstorm. As we stepped into the public plaza, it was filled with bright sunshine and hundreds of people. The building is incredible, but the real eye-opener for me was the setting it created and the open space next to it that people felt so drawn to.'

The Pompidou was one of a small number of special places and spaces that captured Whenray's imagination early on. She grew up in Middlesbrough in the north of England, a town built on steel manufacturing. As a child, Whenray was often surrounded by people who created and made things in their spare time, such as her father, who designed silver jewellery, and her grandfather, who used to carve functional yet beautiful household objects from wood. As a teenager, she showed an aptitude for art and technical drawing, and took evening classes in welding. As Whenray observes, 'I learned a lot about the notion of craft which is inherent in my approach to design and I have always considered architecture to be part of a making process.'

<1. 2.

1. Victoria Whenray at Stadium Place, London 2. Concept sketch, Portobello Square, London

'I believe that the job of an architect is not only to create shelter but to do so in a way that delights and allows the creation of a place where people can flourish.'
– Victoria Whenray

Another design which had a strong influence on Whenray's thinking was the Cummins Engine Factory in Darlington, a 1960s building in glass and steel – and the first in the UK to use Cor-ten – by Eero Saarinen's associates Kevin Roche and John Dinkeloo. 'I fell in love with this elegant and transparent building and its honest expression of structure when I was probably about ten years old', says Whenray, 'although I only discovered its pedigree much later. It was – and still is – a true celebration of industry and gave me a lasting admiration for the international style.'

Whenray enrolled at the School of Architecture at Manchester University, supported by a modest bursary from Middlesbrough Council, which also offered her temporary employment in the in-house architecture department, providing valuable experience in local regeneration projects.

'As a student, I quickly came to realise just how much I love cities and enjoy being in them, discovering and relating to the sense of place they create. I was inspired by how new buildings can be designed to fit so well with much older ones. It was this mix, a juxtaposition of contemporary and historic, which particularly excited me. My first real understanding of this idea was on a field trip to Rome, a city where the layering is so vivid. It's something that has stayed with me ever since.'

Whenray subsequently moved to London where she worked for three different practices and gained expertise across a range of different building types. She began with a studio specialising in conservation projects and worked closely with the Grosvenor Estate on its portfolio of largely listed buildings, later joining the team of project architects on the award-winning Montevetro apartment building designed by Richard Rogers Partnership.

'As an architect, experience is everything', says Whenray, who previously ran her own studio with her partner (who is also an architect) for a number of years. 'It was quite a change moving from listed buildings and understanding how to treat them with respect, to working on a number of contemporary architectural projects and then onto a major regeneration project. This period marked the start of my growing appetite for mixed-used, larger-scale projects.'

In 2010, Whenray joined Conran and Partners, primarily focusing on regeneration, master planning and place-making. 'My first project was Stadium Place in Walthamstow, North London' (see page 22), she says, 'a unique context historically and culturally (it was formerly a dog-racing track), which brings together the broad spectrum of elements that interest me as an architect. It's a large-scale scheme that creates new homes and public spaces while respecting the heritage of the original site, including a number of listed buildings. It embraces a strong community element and offers a unique response to its context and setting. At Walthamstow, it was important that the design included outdoor spaces, each with its own distinctive character, while still incorporating clear elements of an overarching narrative journey.'

Layered, multidimensional projects of this sort connect with Whenray's love of urbanism, place-making and cityscapes. They also connect with her heartfelt belief that good design can – and does – make a difference to people's daily lives, especially when considered within the context of the wider communities they inhabit. 'We should never underestimate the ability of people to appreciate good design', says Whenray, who also serves as an academician at the Academy of Urbanism, a group of like-minded thinkers with a love of the urban environment.

'When I approach a design, I am continually guided by the words of the American poet James Oppenheim, who wrote: "Hearts starve as well as bodies, give us bread, but give us roses." I believe that the job of an architect is not only to create shelter but to do so in a way that delights and allows the creation of a place where people can flourish.'

3. Restored iconic lighting feature at Stadium Place, London **4.** Concept sketch, Portobello Square, London   4.

Stadium Place
Walthamstow, London

The original Walthamstow Stadium, which opened in 1933, was one of London's leading greyhound racing venues for over 70 years. The Art Deco entrance and clock tower became a local landmark and the track hosted champions such as Ballyhennessy Seal and Ballyregan Bob. Winston Churchill addressed an audience of 20,000 people there in 1945 and images of the stadium featured memorably in the CD booklet of Blur's 1994 album *Parklife*. Walthamstow Stadium eventually closed in 2008 and was acquired by the developer London & Quadrant, who approached Conran and Partners to create a master plan and architectural designs for 294 homes on the 1.5-hectare (3.5-acre) stadium site. The homes offer a mixture of private, intermediate and a significant proportion of social housing, as well as a mix of typologies, ranging from one-bed apartments to terraced townhouses.

The £50m project presented a number of challenges. The original stadium was viewed with great affection by the local community, requiring the heritage value of the site to be properly acknowledged in the design approach and amenities provided for use by local people, not just the residents. The new community also needed to connect with the various green spaces close to hand, including a number of local sports grounds. As a result, the design is about making visual connections – not only between different parts of the site but also between the site and the surrounding neighbourhood – and achieving a permeability which had not been possible while the stadium operated as a dog-racing track. The master plan references the historical layout of the stadium to remind residents and visitors of the old footprint of the oval dog track. It is a place with a strong historic and cultural identity. However, there was no existing neighbourhood within the site and the stadium was essentially a closed, inward-looking facility. Conran and Partners set about creating a new neighbourhood from scratch in a way that demonstrated its understanding of and respect for the site's heritage.

Framed views into the development were created to encourage strong connections and reinforce identity, setting up a story for the new community to enjoy. Even the historic finishing line has been embedded into the landscape.

New buildings – expressing a strong architectural language with a distinctive use of materiality and colour echoing the spirit of the Art Deco period of the listed buildings – occupy the sites of the former stands along either side of the piazza area. A sequence of raised flower beds on the site of the old greyhound parade enclosure mark the contours of the former dog track.

As well as the open space provided by the piazza, the master plan includes a number of other communal amenities such as a crèche and a café. The Grade II-listed entrance to the stadium – with its clock tower and tote board – has been preserved and restored. Reglit glass has been used to form two lightweight extensions to the listed tote building to help it function as a contemporary sports amenity. In addition, the geometric design of the new apartments, fronted with profiled metal cladding to give them a monochromatic feel, further references the appearance of the tote building.

At the opposite end of the original stadium sit the dog kennels and two pepperpot huts that once served them. The practice was keen to find fresh uses for this characterful collection of small buildings. 'We talked to the local allotment society as part of our research process and found that it had a 20-year waiting list', Whenray says. 'As a result, we decided to create a series of pocket allotments, using the former dog kennels as potting sheds where users can store implements and other items associated with the maintenance of their plots.' She continues, 'we have, I believe, created a strong sense of place in our design which respects the site's heritage, while supporting the development of a brand new, vibrant community that did not previously exist.'

Conran and Partners' approach has resulted in the opening up of a previously enclosed area and its transformation into part of the wider public domain which can be enjoyed by everyone.

'The master plan we developed references the historical layout of the stadium to remind residents and visitors of the old footprint of the oval dog track.'
– Victoria Whenray

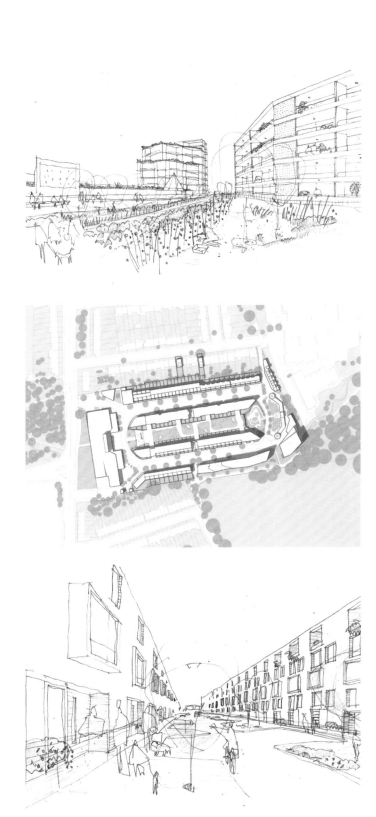

Before enrolling in architecture school, Tim Bowder-Ridger travelled widely across Israel, Egypt and western Turkey, studying and sketching many of the historical and archaeological sites of the region as well as the layering of the modern world in cities such as Jerusalem and Cairo. Experiencing this mixing of cultures and how that is manifested in the design of cities and buildings has shaped his commitment to architecture and design in all its various forms. 'I went into the Hagia Sophia in Istanbul and I knew at that moment that I wanted to be an architect. It was purely an emotional response and it was extraordinary how a building that is 1,500 years old can connect with you so dramatically', says Bowder-Ridger. 'Ancient buildings like this also made me realise the extent to which architecture can have a long-term influence on people's lives. I liked the idea of doing something that could have such a positive and lasting impact on the future.'

Bowder-Ridger went on to study architecture at what is now known as the University of the Creative Arts (UCA) in Canterbury, Kent. The course was deeply rooted in the Bauhaus approach to design. It encouraged students to look at the world from a wide, creative perspective – the school of architecture was directly adjacent to the painting and sculpture schools, and the jewellery and photography facilities. This wider source of inspiration has remained with Bowder-Ridger, reinforced by the influence of his painter wife, Caroline (whom he met early in his studies) and two very creative daughters, themselves now starting on their own journeys.

After graduating from Canterbury, Bowder-Ridger settled in London and began working as an architect at the Douglas Stephen Partnership, initially focusing on the design of primary healthcare buildings that focused very heavily on the ergonomic and emotional needs of the patients as well as the medical staff. He also worked on the design of loft apartments where the focus was creating theatrical but efficient homes that took many of their references from boat design. This period instilled in Bowder-Ridger the discipline of thinking carefully about how people use spaces functionally, but also about the aspirations for those spaces. After joining Conran and Partners in 1997 and initially delivering a boutique hotel (MyHotel Bloomsbury, London), Bowder-Ridger quickly went on to work directly with Terence Conran, at a time when he was rapidly expanding his restaurant empire.

'Terence has influenced me more than anybody else in my professional life. He made it clear from the outset who a project was for – the end-user. This means taking a fundamentally humane approach to architecture and design that addresses both functional and emotional needs', says Bowder-Ridger. 'This approach requires an understanding of when to elaborate and perhaps create a sense of theatre, and when to introduce a sense of quiet calm through the use of volume, light and materiality. It is about forming a landscape that draws people through, making complicated problems seemingly simple to resolve. It is about designing buildings and spaces that are fundamentally at ease with themselves in a way that is tangible and accessible to users.'

As an entrepreneur, Terence would regularly note that creativity must work with commercial success, not against it. Consistently the practice's most successful projects have been those where there is a mutual understanding of this basic but very important principle.

Bowder-Ridger subsequently focused on residential and hotel projects in the UK and overseas, enabling him to work simultaneously as an interior designer as well as an architect and evolve his skill-set as a designer of complete buildings. This journey has culminated in the recent completion of Centre Point Tower (see page 33), a project where Mike Hussey – founder of London developer Almacantar – required the practice to approach the reinterpretation of this iconic but long-ignored and previously deteriorating building in a very layered way. The design – which has created a stunning residential development from a former office tower – needed to reconnect with the original spirit of the building while making sure it became relevant to future generations. Bowder-Ridger's complete-building approach encompassed not solely the structure itself but styling of the key spaces and a collaboration with the building's branding team to complete the story – a brief that is rarely offered to most contemporary architectural practices. As Bowder-Ridger explains, 'this project is a great example of where we have been given a very clear brief by a client which we have then developed into a design narrative that the whole collaborative team has taken ownership of and delivered with astonishing consistency across an eight-year project duration. It is an exemplar of the old cliché that your projects can only be as good as your client.

'Opening a studio in Hong Kong in 2017 was our response to extending access to a maturing market, a widening talent pool and an exciting cultural context. We will certainly be seeking to continue to grow our international work and explore new markets going forward, but we have no plans to become a 'super-size practice', and we want to ensure, as a group of like-minded partners, that our fundamental studio approach and ethos is maintained.'

'It is about designing buildings and spaces that are fundamentally at ease with themselves in a way that is tangible and accessible to users.'
— Tim Bowder-Ridger

Centre Point Tower
Central London

Ever since its completion in 1966, Centre Point Tower has been a landmark on the London skyline, situated alongside the junction of Oxford Street, Tottenham Court Road and Charing Cross Road. The tower was the most original and characterful of a series of mid-century buildings designed by Richard Seifert and his partner George Marsh. It is defined by its elegant profile and its innovative exterior frame – made of precast, structural concrete components – which lends the building a dynamic quality.

Centre Point Tower was originally designed and built as an office building. Following its acquisition by the developer Almacantar, Conran and Partners was approached to work on the adaptive reuse and reinvention of the building, converting the tower to residential use. Arranged over 34 floors, the building now features 82 apartments, including a duplex penthouse at its summit. These are all supported by amenities more commonly found within luxury hotels or private members' clubs and include a 30m swimming pool, a gym, spa treatment rooms, a club lounge and a cinema. A private dining room has been provided and equipped with a full catering kitchen, enabling residents to extend their apartment spaces when required for the purposes of entertaining guests.

'The overarching architectural approach was to work with the building itself. For people who didn't know what Centre Point Tower was really like before, we wanted them to believe that this is the way that it has always been. For people who did know, we wanted them to believe that this is how it always should have been', says Bowder-Ridger.

Within R. Seifert & Partners' original design for Centre Point Tower – which sculptor Eduardo Paolozzi described as London's first pop art building – the ground floor was an open undercroft that formed part of the complex maze of vehicular and pedestrian traffic buzzing around the base of the skyscraper. Following the re-routing of the original gyratory and a redesign of the surrounding streetscape by MICA Architects (also responsible for reworking the lower, lateral building alongside Centre Point Tower), Conran and Partners was able to take back the ground plane and create an entrance and glazed vestibule, connecting with a generous new public square. From this semi-transparent entrance plane, one steps upwards – via the restored and relocated twin staircases – to the mezzanine gallery, which forms part of a buffer zone for residents between the busy streetscape and the private realm.

'One of the key questions that needed to be addressed was how do you connect, as a resident, with the hustle and bustle of the city but on your own terms?' says Bowder-Ridger.

'In response, a journey was created from the public realm at street level to the semi-private ground floor to the mezzanine and upwards. By the time you reach the level of the first apartments – at the equivalent of the building's fifth storey – you feel very protected and you become an observer looking down on the city below. You have panoramic views from floor ten but even on those lower floors you are still floating above the streetscape and the traffic with a generous new pedestrian square.'

Whilst little of the internal finishes had survived over the years, the practice was able to save and restore the exposed structural concrete, the bespoke tiled columns at the base of the building and an area of delightful marble inlaid terrazzo on the mezzanine, plus the handrails in the escape stairs climbing the full 100 metres of the building. Otherwise all the internal and external finishes were new insertions, albeit designed to sit naturally with the spirit of the building and, in the case of the new thermal and acoustic glazing, following the pattern of the original.

Circulation and service spaces are positioned at the centre of the floor plan, allowing the living rooms and bedrooms around the periphery to enjoy open vistas across London and a striking quality of natural light; hidden blinds avoid the need for curtains on the newly installed windows, while a light restoration process has brought out the patina of the original concrete framework. The apartments themselves range in size and scale from one-bedroom flats to four-bedroom whole-floor apartments towards the top of the tower. Whilst the configuration and the specifications naturally vary as the apartments grow in size, all enjoy equal access to the amenity spaces and spectacular views across the newly created streetscape and across London. Crowning the building is a five-bedroom duplex on the uppermost two floors, created by the removal of the original water tanks and other services, which is – in effect – a grand house in the sky.

Every habitable room has at least two windows, which really enabled the design to engage with the key modernist priorities of light and air, while also creating a feeling of generosity within these spaces. Bowder-Ridger says, 'our approach celebrates the sense of space and makes the most of the building's unique qualities, so that it becomes an experience. We are always trying to remind you that you are in Centre Point, so the ironmongery – for instance – is bespoke to the project, along with much of the detailing.'

There is a subtle mid-century influence throughout. Materials for the interior finishes are largely natural, including oak for the fitted wardrobes and storage units, as well as French limestone tiles for the entrance halls, whilst the central spaces adopt darker materials, contrasting with the blonde palette in the main living spaces and bedrooms. The living rooms are open plan, with zones for seating and dining, whilst lightly connecting with galley kitchens towards the centre. In this way, the key emphasis always remains the vista, which stretches all the way across London.

'We have designed a tranquil oasis in what is, otherwise, a very busy part of the capital while maximising the uninterrupted views', says Bowder-Ridger. 'Where we have made changes, we have tried to make sure they feel like natural changes that sit comfortably within the scheme as a whole. It allowed us to apply our expertise in the hospitality sector to shape a residential development which reflects how people wish to live today.'

The environmental performance of the building has been significantly enhanced, an approach that is at once both environmentally and culturally sustainable.

'Our approach celebrates the sense of space and making the most of
the advantages of the building, so that it becomes an experience.'
— Tim Bowder-Ridger

Kita Aoyama
Tokyo

The concept for this high-quality residential development was inspired by a woodblock print by Katsushika Hokusai entitled 'Cushion Pine at Aoyama'. From the series 'Thirty-six Views of Mount Fuji', the print was created when the area was a green landscape traditionally occupied by the Samurai. It has since become a highly urbanised neighbourhood within the heart of the bustling metropolis. The design references the print through the building's form and its use of natural stone. By including a series of generously landscaped terraces, Conran and Partners has sought to return something of the original rural landscape of the area.

The seven-storey development of 15 apartments for NTT Urban Development, in one of Tokyo's most fashionable areas, responds to its immediate built context in terms of scale and massing, while offering a unique addition to the location. The densely planted, fair-faced concrete and flamed-granite ziggurat structure references the spirit of the Hokusai print, but also creates a green stepping stone within one of the great megacities of the world. The emphasis on native planting by landscape architect Tatsuya Hiraga allows nature to return to the city, enhancing and repairing the quality of the local neighbourhood.

This project encapsulates a holistic approach through its architecture and interior design, linked by the spaces which run between the various elements of the development, internally and externally. The result is an overall spatial experience, creating a continuous journey from the street to the home through a hierarchy of spaces and layers.

The apartments are unusually large for Tokyo, recognising the cultural sensitivities in terms of separating reception spaces and private spaces such as bedrooms and bathrooms. This is manifested by public and private circulation routes and zones within apartments. This understanding of cultural needs is further recognised by embracing classic Japanese hospitality. The generously proportioned entrance halls ('genkan') are designed to accommodate the Japanese welcome ritual, where guests are greeted and shoes removed before they are led into the main habitable spaces. Each step of this process is identified by passing through timber portals and transitioning from one material to another, in a sequence that echoes the thresholds of traditional Japanese homes.

Both the living spaces and bedrooms offer timber-framed views of the planted terraces, referencing the inspiration of the Hokusai 'cushion pine' concept. Winter gardens provide a transitional space between internal and exterior areas, with granite paving providing a visual linking motif. Bowder-Ridger says, 'our approach is a focused response to the physical, historical and cultural context of the location, making this tangible for the end-users with a view to creating a definitive sense of place.'

'Our approach is a focused response to the physical, historical and cultural context of the location, making this tangible for the end-users with a view to creating a definitive sense of place.'
– Tim Bowder-Ridger

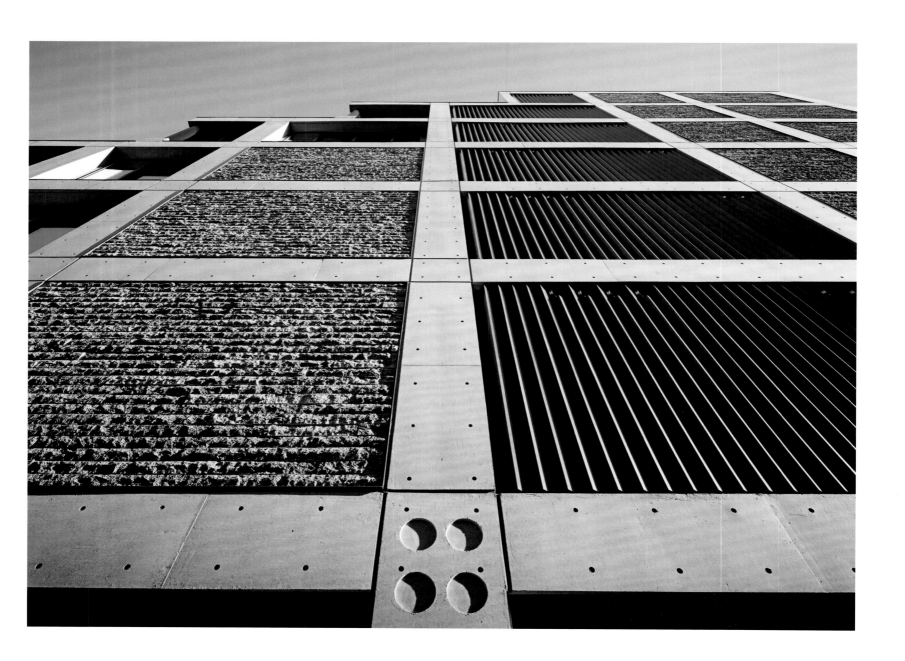

City Lofts
Manchester & Sheffield

Conran and Partners worked with developer City Lofts for over a decade from the early 2000s. It was a time when similar brands such as Urban Splash, Yoo and Manhattan Lofts were converting former industrial premises and building new projects to address the growing need for well-designed, urban living spaces. City Lofts focused on delivering significant apartment schemes in key regional cities, collaborating with Conran and Partners to focus primarily on compact, modern and inviting apartments.

Conran and Partners' long-term relationship with City Lofts allowed them to refine the product in terms of the planning and interiors, while providing them with striking architecture. The projects focused on delivering high-quality, well-insulated, entry-level housing in out-of-London locations. City Lofts' apartments were very much aimed at the rental market, particularly younger renters who were likely to move between a number of different spaces in their early years, and unlikely to want to put down roots too soon. The company adopted a buy-to-rent approach far ahead of this type of housing development becoming more widespread in the UK. However, older down-sizers also moved in, selling their large family homes in favour of the attractions of modern city living and the proximity of shops, restaurants and cultural activities.

Key Conran and Partners' projects include Salford Quays – adjacent to Media City, near Manchester – which was given a distinctive character with timber-faced cladding. Another scheme, Quayside Lofts in Newcastle, comprises three simple, robust brick buildings based around the historic Tuthill Stairs that run down from the castle to the riverside. In central Manchester, 38 High Street utilises a shimmering, aubergine-coloured glazed terracotta tile that adapts to the Manchester climate beautifully, while Vantage Quay in Piccadilly Basin incorporates a tough red-brick elevation that references the industrial buildings in the surrounding streets combined with a softer approach on its water-facing side, using render with an expressed timber screen. St Paul's Tower in Sheffield – comprising two linked residential buildings with commercial and public spaces – is the tallest building in the city. Part of the 'Heart of the City' project, this 31-storey tower with 322 apartments and ground-floor retail space uses a local sandstone cladding and bronzed metal to give a warmth and richness to the scheme.

A sense of spatial generosity was key to the approach on these projects, even though the individual apartments needed to be compact at 45–65 sq m. For instance, bedrooms can be opened out to living rooms, omitting corridors and creating a frontage that feels like a single, linear space. Furthermore, in two-bedroom apartments, one bedroom incorporates an en suite, whilst the shared bathroom is directly adjacent to the other bedroom. This allows occupiers enhanced levels of privacy, a key factor in designing even the smallest of homes, particularly for those sharing an apartment.

Kitchens and bathrooms were manufactured off-site using a highly efficient and cost-effective production and delivery process. This enabled quality finishes and crisp detailing to be brought up to a level normally very difficult to achieve on site. As Tim Bowder-Ridger observes, 'we sought to imbue these buildings with a sense of place, creating an identity that relates to the specific contexts of the sites. For example, the warehouse massing and the choices of specific red-brick and timber finishes were used on Vantage Quay to provide material references to tone of the Manchester canal side context. We also designed a range of interior specifications that were intended to stand above the usual developer fit-out. As with our current residential work, we design from the inside out – residents spend most of the time experiencing the interiors – and then back in again.'

'We always sought to bring a sense of character across these various buildings,
 creating an identity that relates to the specific contexts of the sites.'
— Tim Bowder-Ridger

Blake Tower
Barbican, London

Situated on the edge of London's Barbican Estate, Blake Tower is the fourth skyscraper within this much-admired brutalist enclave. One of the most successful examples of large-scale, post-war British architecture – with its unique mix of residential elements, cultural centre and outdoor spaces – the Barbican Estate was designed by architects Chamberlin, Powell & Bon and is Grade II listed. One of the four original towers served as a YMCA youth hostel. When the YMCA moved out of the building, developer Redrow London asked Conran and Partners to convert it to residential use, giving buyers the first opportunity in decades to acquire a 'new' Barbican apartment.

The distinctive 17-storey tower was originally designed with modestly scaled guest rooms for students and other short-stay visitors. The conversion involved creating more generous and inviting apartments better suited for modern living, ranging in size from studios and one-bedroom flats up to three-bedroom apartments and two penthouses. The redesign has been delivered within the existing structural and façade grids of the building. Like Centre Point Tower (see page 33), the design approach needed to make the most of the views and the ready-made advantages of the building itself. Given the Barbican's context, the design approach also needed to reference the unique character of the neighbouring estate. Being part of the Barbican and an important brutalist building meant there was a very rich source of creative inspiration to draw upon.

The form – in precast engineered sculptural concrete – and original materiality, including concrete, terrazzo, brass and ceramic tiles, were exceptional. Conran and Partners wanted the new apartments to have a personality that worked with and respected the context, without being too brutal or extreme. The practice's approach therefore sought to lighten it up and add warmth to make sure that the tower and the homes within it felt welcoming to residents and their guests.

The old, cellular spaces were stripped away and the tower reconfigured floor by floor. The modern heritage of the Barbican is referenced in the use of exposed, pick-hammered concrete in hallways and circulation zones, but there are also timber floors, wooden doors and joinery, along with other overtly domestic textures. The intelligent spatial planning of the original Barbican apartments has been echoed through the use of space-saving kitchen designs, alongside many fitted elements including window seats, wardrobes and storage cupboards. These help enhance the sense of space and encourage the flow of light.

Simon Kincaid says, 'there are some elements, such as the tilework used in the bathrooms and lobby areas, which draw on the graphic nature of the mid-century period. We adopted a confident approach to reinforce the spirit of the building, not least because we anticipated that the kind of people who will be drawn to Blake Tower would want to connect strongly with the Barbican iconography and aesthetic.'

The lobby itself features a custom, brass-inlaid screen to one side with an abstract pattern, as well as terrazzo floors and an integrated, fitted bench that fluidly morphs into the concierge's desk. Splashes of colour contrast with a relatively light palette. The interior treatment of both communal and private spaces needed to feel in keeping with the spirit of the original building. The bathrooms – with their bespoke, crafted vanity units – are a key design feature which reference the originals.

'Brutalism was all about the expression of structure. So, in the true spirit of the brutalist movement, the apartments have been strategically designed to reveal the building's original architectural anatomy', says Kincaid. Conran and Partners' design has sought to soften the interiors while retaining the cold, hard materials from the modernist period. This relationship aims to give the residences a clear identity while ensuring an element of authenticity.

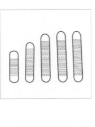

'In the true spirit of the brutalist movement, the apartments have been strategically designed to reveal the building's original architectural anatomy'
– Simon Kincaid

Gabriel Square
St Albans

The city of St Albans has many advantages as a residential quarter. It has a charm and character of its own, with a provenance that stretches back to Roman times. Bordered by green belt, yet also just beyond the outer edge of London, it is a short journey from the centre of the capital. This makes it a desirable destination for those seeking to relocate out of London. For Conran and Partners, commissioned to design the interiors for a series of townhouses and apartments at Gabriel Square, it represented a fresh contextual challenge in a number of different respects.

The development, by Meyer Homes, consists of 52 townhouses and 28 apartments arranged around a new, generously landscaped garden square. This square helps to define the identity of the development as a whole, providing a large communal garden that offers a tempting amenity in itself. This is complemented by a sequence of gardens, balconies, terraces and roof terraces that offer a whole range of public and private outdoor spaces. 'The interiors needed to respond to the setting and reinforce the relationships between indoor and outdoor space. A sense of transparency and simplicity was vital', says Simon Kincaid.

The four-storey townhouses are based on a relatively tall and narrow plan. As well as establishing a vivid relationship between inside and outside, the interiors seek to forge lateral and vertical connections that tie different levels together, as well as enhancing the quality of natural light throughout. This approach has resulted in the creation of modern, open homes within a townhouse typology that contrasts with traditional cellular living and aims to bring apartment design into a townhouse setting.

The layouts were reconfigured to accommodate a top-floor master-suite with bedrooms facing onto the square, a walk-in wardrobe and a bathroom with a freestanding bath, walk-in shower and a direct connection to the private roof terrace. This offers occupiers something akin to a penthouse experience, emphasising the sense of modernity and generosity of spaces compared with the traditional housing stock typical of the area.

Circulation routes are wide and generous, creating a fluid relationship between the key living spaces that enhances the sense of volume and connectivity. Staircases double as lightwells, bringing sunlight deep into the heart of the homes. A number of townhouses also incorporate double-height kitchens, emphasising the volume and creating playful volumetric shifts and surprises. A soft, calming palette of materials was chosen, with oak staircases and flooring in the main living spaces. Pale tones are deployed throughout, with subtle textural shifts. Bush-hammered limestone tiles in the bathrooms provide texture and contrast, while maintaining an emphasis on a light, bright spectrum of colours. This finish references the stone of the development itself, as well as the limestone used to construct the city's cathedral.

The apartments – which range from one- to four-bedrooms – explore similar themes within a more limited footprint. Here, too, connections with outdoor space and the garden square help to liberate the interiors. 'While the townhouses feature a calm, purist aesthetic, the apartments have a subtle mid-century modern influence throughout, typified by more graphic and youthful design touches', says Kincaid.

'While the townhouses feature a calm, purist aesthetic, the apartments have a subtle mid-century modern influence throughout, typified by more graphic and youthful design touches.'
– Simon Kincaid

LUMA
King's Cross, London

The redevelopment of the King's Cross estate, to the north of the railway station, has seen the evolution of an extraordinary sequence of buildings which form part of one of the largest urban quarters delivered in central London in decades. Argent, the developer of this new 'campus', invited contributions from a range of leading UK and international architects and designers, commissioning Conran and Partners to work on the interior design of a number of spaces including LUMA, a new residential building with architecture by Squire & Partners.

The building consists of two stepped blocks, one of them arranged across ten floors and the other across seven, with just over 60 apartments in total. LUMA, from both its eastern- and western-facing sides, overlooks two parks which are key communal outdoor spaces in the Argent development. These areas of public realm help to create a sense of openness for residents as well as enhancing the quality of light inside the apartments. This strong visual connection to the parks, combined with the dual aspect of many apartments, gives LUMA a distinctive feel of urban luxury.

Similar to other developments across the King's Cross estate, LUMA is a truly collaborative project – yet it still holds a very strong identity of its own. Conran and Partners designed the communal spaces and apartments around the idea of an urban escape within the city – with an aesthetic that references spas, hotels and even private members' clubs.

The graphic pattern of the metallic brise soleil on the façade references the pattern of dappled light that forms when sunlight filters through a tree canopy. This effect is replicated throughout the apartment spaces as light passes through the screens and into the rooms. A similar design motif is repeated in the communal lobby, where latticed screens subtly partition the main reception from a lounge area, which features additional spaces for meetings or relaxation. 'The interiors here draw on Conran and Partners' experience in the hospitality sector, offering a welcoming and multilayered reception area', says Kincaid. 'The transition from outside to inside is soft and natural. There's a relationship between the external and internal spaces which is reinforced by the connections through to the parks on either side, whilst the synergy between these spaces enables the overall development to feel more open, generous and engaging.'

The interior design of the apartments also makes the most of these connections, drawing upon the park views and rich quality of natural light. Apartments range in scale from one- to three-bedrooms, as well as penthouses, and include many multilevel and dual-aspect homes which have become the signature units of the development.

Setting LUMA apart from others within the King's Cross estate, some apartments have been designed with exceptionally generous ceiling heights and split-level living spaces to enhance the overall sense of space and give a distinctive quality, completed with a light material palette that uses pale joinery and stonework. Key living spaces are oriented towards the tall windows and balconies, while fitted bookcases and storage ensure clean lines throughout. To reinforce the calm aesthetic, timber panelling has been used to conceal kitchen utilities, a detail repeated in the design of the bathroom and hallway spaces.

'Each project we undertake has its own special story and sense of place', says Kincaid. 'With LUMA, we have focused on using finishes and materials that are deliberately understated, natural and refined. It is a purposefully soft palette that works well in this setting. Yet it's also about creating a sense of identity and character for the apartments themselves, which references some of our other work, particularly with hotels. These apartments have been described as having the feel of a collection of bespoke residences despite there being more than 60 separate units in the development.'

The Lighterman and The Waterman
Greenwich, London

The regeneration of the Greenwich Peninsula represents one of the most ambitious urban projects in London for many years.

Within the phased master plan to deliver this fresh community, Conran and Partners was asked by developer Knight Dragon to work on the design of two new residential towers within the Lower Riverside quarter of the peninsula. The two towers – known as The Lighterman and The Waterman – are punctuated by communal courtyards, plazas and landscaped spaces at ground level, while the apartments offer views across the river and to the city beyond. 'One of the key challenges, given that the two towers sit next to one another, was to develop an architectural language for each one that was kindred in spirit but different enough to create a sense of character for them both', says Tina Norden. 'To achieve this, we developed two different approaches with shifts in tone and articulation so that they each express themselves in a unique way.'

Norden and her team began collaborating with Pilbrow & Partners and Carey Jones Chapman Tolcher, the two architectural practices working on the towers, at an early stage. This helped in the evolution not only of the apartments themselves but also the communal spaces and amenities within the towers. 'Because of our combined architectural and interiors background, one of the things that we pride ourselves on at Conran and Partners is our understanding of spatial planning and getting the best out of a layout to make sure that it really works for people's lives within these homes', says Norden.

While drawing inspiration from the history and context of Greenwich itself, as well as the riverside setting, the interior treatment of the two towers evolved in parallel. The Waterman adopts contrasting tones within a textural palette of light and dark shades, while introducing materials and finishes such as brass and ironwork that reference the industrial history of the peninsula. The Lighterman adopts a softer, tonal approach in terms of its colours and finishes, whilst similarly offering a bold contemporary character. Both towers have spacious, substantial and inviting lobbies that reference hotel lobby design. They include communal seating areas and meeting spaces, as well as striking open volumes and statement lighting. Here, as elsewhere in Conran and Partners' residential portfolio, the lobbies help set the atmosphere and identity of the building, while also providing clear orientation for residents and guests accessing social amenities such as coffee bars, screening rooms and libraries.

The design of the apartments – within a range of scales from studios to penthouses – provides elements such as bespoke kitchens, luxurious bathrooms and integrated storage within an aesthetic suited to the overall building design as well as contemporary living standards and requirements. In particular, the penthouses offered an opportunity to work at a more dramatic scale. The Waterman penthouse, for example, features a double-height living space arranged around a marble-clad fireplace and open views of the whole city across the Thames and Canary Wharf, while a mezzanine gallery hosts a library and study. 'The penthouses are fabulous in the way they pick up on the different characteristics seen in the two buildings', says Norden.

The Waterman penthouse is very three-dimensional and explores the tonal contrasts between the black and the white, while The Lighterman penthouse is single storey, over the whole floor level, with a more tonal and delicate palette but incorporating dramatic elements like a floating feature fireplace and statement kitchen.

The two buildings were part of the first phase of the ambitious master plan of the area and were extremely successful in their sales. This development set the level of quality and ambition for the site and Greenwich Peninsula is now becoming the vibrant neighbourhood that Knight Dragon envisaged from the outset.

Pleasure

The world of leisure has changed rapidly and profoundly over recent years, in part enabled by the digital world. This shift in culture sits very comfortably with Conran and Partners' long-standing reputation as being lifestyle designers, with a strong tradition, encouraged by Terence Conran, of considering how people want to behave rather than forcing them into artificially compartmentalised lives as with previous generations. In parallel to this shift, people's expectations are becoming greater. For instance, as people are more widely travelled, hotels have become increasingly sophisticated, offering a range of experiences; restaurants have had to reinvent themselves in a highly competitive marketplace where there is an expectation of authenticity; and retail premises have seen extraordinary changes and challenges over the past decade, as traditional stores seek to find their place within a world of online shopping and home delivery.

Conran and Partners has been involved in hotel design for many years, exploring new ideas and embracing new influences. Just as hotel design has played a part in influencing residential design, as we saw in the previous section of this book, the same is true in reverse, with many new hotels adopting a more domestic, relaxed and comfortable aesthetic. At the same time, residential amenities such as spas, pools and other leisure facilities are becoming increasingly elaborate. As Tim Bowder-Ridger observes, 'our starting point is always to thoroughly research the location, the architecture, the city and its history – everything within the environs of the project. Onto this, we layer the type of hotel and its operational style, as well as the ambitions and the brief of owners and/or operators. We then develop a narrative which forms the basis of our design approach and is something we continue to reference with the client again and again. The whole team needs to buy into the concept so that it becomes the touchstone for the project.'

This framework clearly has to fit the brief and programme, as well as relating closely to the brand values and identity of the hotel group in question. Increasingly, the larger hospitality chains are demanding highly individual and contextual design concepts, current examples including two bespoke and very distinctive luxury hotels in Auckland, New Zealand, and Jakarta, Indonesia, both for the Park Hyatt brand, but with their own personalities (see page 100). The practice has also helped to design entirely new hotel concepts, including the QO in Amsterdam for the InterContinental Hotels Group (see page 89), which has been conceived and created with a positive and ambitious focus on sustainability.

1. Park Hyatt Hotel, Jakarta **2.** Boundary, London

In addition, Conran and Partners has also worked on many smaller, boutique hotels, including PURO Kazimierz in Kraków (see page 107), where the residential influence is very apparent, and the emphasis is upon the curation of engaging home-from-home retreats and less on communal amenities. The design of both the South Place Hotel (see page 83) and the Boundary (see page 163) in London sit within the context of a particularly strong food offer, with a range of restaurants and bars which anchor the projects just as much – if not more so – as the guest rooms themselves.

Certainly, the overlap between hotel and restaurant design is very fluid for the practice. Clearly, as noted in the general introduction, restaurant design forms a key part of the heritage of the practice itself, with a broad portfolio of projects driven by vivid narratives and distinctive food concepts. What distinguishes the practice is the innate understanding of operational and functional aspects layered onto the creative ability which comes from the history of the group as restaurant owners and operators. This continues today with projects such as the German Gymnasium in London (see page 77), and with projects further afield, such as Rüya in Dubai, which involved the creation of an aesthetic brand language that could be carried over to other new restaurants under the same name, including an eatery in London's Mayfair.

Increasingly, high street or shopping mall retail stores are becoming experiential showcases for a brand and its products. This approach is manifested in the practice's design for KEF in Hong Kong (see page 97), which deliberately eschews the normal feel of a speaker store, where the technology would typically dominate at the cost of understanding how it translates into the home. In fact, this project has the feel of a club, with a tangible domestic atmosphere.

As well as concept stores such as KEF, Conran and Partners is actively exploring new retail concepts including The Life in South Korea (see page 117) and crossover projects such as the Boundary, which combines elements of retail, food and drink and hospitality all in one location. This overlapping of uses and the focus on experience, or even theatre, has been a core feature of hospitality design for some time and is now becoming a key component of retail and restaurant projects too. Interestingly, it is also increasingly regarded as an important factor in mainstream workplace design, whereas it was previously limited to the creative sector (see 200 Gray's Inn Road, page 166). Conran and Partners, with its proven credentials across all these sectors, is perfectly placed to respond to these changing requirements. 'As a practice we design ways of living', says Tim Bowder-Ridger. 'But for us, the Venn diagrams of project types are overlapping more and more.'

Portrait: Tina Norden

Tina Norden always knew that she wanted a life in design – and it was not only because of her early obsession with Lego. She grew up on the outskirts of the German port city of Hamburg. Like many industrial and maritime cities, Hamburg had established itself over the centuries as a creative, cultural and commercial hub with a liberal, free-thinking culture which hugely influenced Norden's formative years.

From an early age she was inspired by the work of her late father, a landscape architect who ran his own practice in the city. 'I remember going to some of the big projects he was involved in, including the Planten un Blomen park in the centre of Hamburg', says Norden. 'Even when I was very little, my father would encourage me to accompany him to client meetings and visit some of the schemes he was working on. I was at my happiest with crayons and a layout plan sitting in a corner of his office. It gave me an early insight into the design process.'

As well as having an interest in design, Norden was a good linguist and took part in several exchange programmes, including one with Oundle School in Northamptonshire, UK, as a teenager. She toyed with the idea of becoming a diplomat as it would indulge her passion for languages and travel. Architecture won her over however and, after spending a year out in London directly after leaving school, she decided to apply to study the discipline in the UK. 'I came over to London at the age of 18 and never really left', says Norden. 'I fell in love with the city because it was so vibrant and open-minded. You could be whoever you wanted to be and there were so many exciting things going on. I was drawn to its incredible music scene, which continues to have a huge influence on my thinking as a designer – I even ended up marrying a musician. When it came to applying for university, London was the only place I wanted to be. The fact that I was offered places at several different institutions based on my hastily assembled portfolio convinced me that I had made the right choice.'

<1. 2.

1. Tina Norden at German Gymnasium, London 2. Anatolian restaurant Rüya, Dubai 3. Maximilian Hotel guest room, Prague

'We don't have a set house style. Instead, we have a narrative and research driven approach to design that allows us to develop each project as a unique response to the brief, the client and the setting.'
– Tina Norden

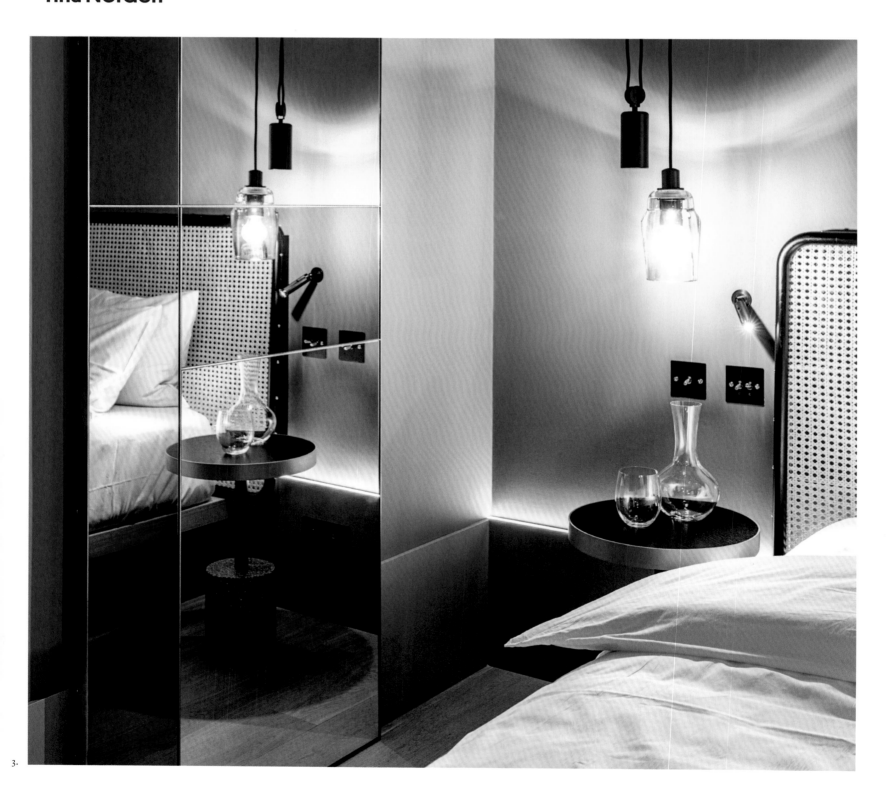

Once she had started studying for her BA at the University of Westminster, it suited Norden that the course offered her an arts-based, creative approach to architecture. A key influence while there was her tutor, Allen Cunningham, who had worked in practice with Marcel Breuer in New York before being appointed Head of Architecture at Westminster. Cunningham helped to encourage Norden's growing love of modernist architecture, becoming a mentor and also instrumental in organising a summer work placement for her in New York. After completing Part I, Norden's year out led her to a placement at Conran and Partners. 'I had a feeling straight away that it was the right place for me', Norden says.

During the placement Norden worked on a bar project in Iceland and collaborated on a large architectural scheme in Japan, opening her mind to interior design as well as architecture. Until then, she had been focused on the pure architecture route at Westminster. Realising that her design interests were a lot broader, she decided to apply to the Royal College of Art (RCA) in London, which at the time offered a unique combined architecture and interiors Masters course. Here Norden completed her Part II, as well as exploring her interest in interior architecture and the many other design disciplines being taught there.

Two key figures at the RCA at that time were architects Nigel Coates and David Adjaye, both of whom influenced Norden's approach to design and interiors. Coates played the part of agent provocateur, encouraging his students to think outside the box. Adjaye was, at that time, involved in a series of innovative residential projects for artists and fashion designers that spliced architecture and highly crafted, original interior spaces. While studying at the RCA, Norden had continued working at Conran and Partners several days a week. By the time she graduated, it was a natural choice to return to the practice full time.

'From the very outset, I felt that I had a high degree of creative freedom at Conran and Partners', says Norden. 'There is a sensibility and an approach to design that we all share. However, the outcomes are very different for each project and it's up to us, as partners, to develop new ideas which still fit with the overall ethos of the practice. It's about being a creative collective in the best sense of the term.'

In her early years, Norden assumed responsibility for the restaurant projects, working closely with Terence Conran on a number of high-profile schemes. These were narrative-driven with strong storylines, including Skylon at the Royal Festival Hall, a particular favourite of hers. 'Terence is a very intuitive yet practical designer', Norden says. 'I was influenced by the fact that, as a restaurateur himself, he focused on the function of spaces as well as on the experience a restaurant offers diners. He has a real eye for introducing unique, quirky touches that stay in guests' minds. Skylon was an emotive project and a joy to work on, not just because of its incredible space but also because of its location in one of London's most iconic buildings.'

Other key projects for Norden include the German Gymnasium restaurant in King's Cross, London (see page 77), with a narrative referencing its vibrant history and echoes of her own German heritage, and the South Place Hotel, Finsbury, London (see page 83), a formative first opportunity to lead on a large-scale hotel project. Norden went on to work on numerous restaurant and hotel projects including the Maximilian in Prague (see page 93) and two landmark Park Hyatt hotels in Auckland and Jakarta (see page 100), each with its own distinctive aesthetic.

'The two Park Hyatt hotels perfectly demonstrate that we don't have a set house style. Instead, we have a narrative and research-driven approach to design that allows us to develop each project as a unique response to the brief, the client and the setting', says Norden.

German Gymnasium
King's Cross, London

Among the many shining examples of new-build, 21st-century architecture across Argent's regenerated 'campus' around King's Cross Station, the German Gymnasium stands out proudly. It is one of three key period listed buildings here (Gasholders and Coal Drops Yard being the other two) and one of the first to be reinvented and given a fresh lease of life within the King's Cross master plan.

Its history stretches back to the 1860s, when a group of German émigrés founded this spacious temple to exercise and well-being. The triple-height exercise hall was spanned overhead by supporting arches made of laminated timber, while mezzanine galleries allowed visitors to look down upon the vigorous activities going on below. The sheer scale of the gymnasium was, in a way, an echo of the vast train stations to either side of it, namely King's Cross and St Pancras.

During the First World War, the building was damaged by a Zeppelin strike and more damage was done by later conversions that carved up the gym into offices. But then the restaurant group D&D London – with whom Conran and Partners has worked many times over – was asked by Argent to join them in creating an extraordinary new restaurant inspired by the great eateries of Central Europe. 'The German Gymnasium is a project that is very close to my heart in many ways', says Tina Norden. 'I was born in Germany, so there is obviously a personal link, and it is an important reminder of a fascinating period of history. It is a fabulous building and we were fortunate to be involved with the project very early on, helping to turn the gym into something that could function as a landmark restaurant in a part of London that has been totally reinvented.'

Working closely with Argent (a developer with which the practice has collaborated on several projects in the King's Cross campus) and their base-build architect Allies and Morrison, Conran and Partners developed ideas that focused on reconfiguring everything within the shell of the building to allow it to function as a hospitality space; the reinstatement of the open grandeur of the great hall combined with all of the amenities of an ambitious 21st-century restaurant. The triple-height volume of the gym was revealed again, including the striking ceiling and its supporting arches. The concept of a mezzanine gallery running around the open hallway was also revived.

The practice sought to open up the original building so that when visitors walk in they are greeted with an amazing sense of space and volume beneath a highly distinctive ceiling. All the functional spaces are located at one end: the kitchens, service areas stacked on top of each other with an invisible mezzanine. The approach was about making practical sense out of the building and getting it to work as a modern restaurant, whilst also preserving and enhancing its original character.

The main restaurant and bar are at ground level, with the seating carefully zoned to create a choice of experiences within the space. Dramatic new twin staircases ascend to the mezzanine level, which offers more intimate dining, a cocktail bar and private areas. From the gallery, guests can look down as well as up, allowing them to savour the theatrical scale of the former gym. 'Elements like the staircases are super contemporary, along with the other interventions, so you can clearly distinguish the old and the new insertions', Norden says. 'Subtle references to the heritage of the gymnasium were also introduced – the floor, for instance, has markings reminiscent of a sports hall, but picked out in marble, and not to forget the playful graphics in the bathrooms. We worked very hard on the spatial planning and layout, trying to do as much as we could with the building while respecting its personality and spirit.'

'It is a fabulous building and we were fortunate to be involved with the project very early on, helping to turn the gym into something that could function as a landmark restaurant in a part of London that has been totally reinvented.'
– Tina Norden

South Place Hotel
City of London

Conran and Partners has a long working relationship with the innovative and influential restaurant group D&D London. This ongoing collaboration has encompassed many projects including the German Gymnasium restaurant in King's Cross (see page 77) and New Street Grill and Old Bengal Bar in the Old Bengal Warehouse development near Liverpool Street (see page 121). South Place Hotel, in the City of London, marked the first hotel in the D&D portfolio and a fresh design challenge in which gastronomy plays a key part.

South Place can be seen as a series of restaurants with rooms rather than a traditional hotel, so the ground floor comprises restaurants and bars, with another restaurant on the rooftop. The first floor includes uniquely designed private dining rooms as well as offering a gym and spa. The whole experience is aimed at a sophisticated city audience, but the practice wanted to create something that felt different to anything else that you might find there, drawing people in with a relaxed yet refined atmosphere.

The building itself was a bespoke new addition to the neighbourhood, with the shell and structure designed by architect Allies and Morrison. As interior architects, Conran and Partners began working closely with the architect at an early stage, shaping the internal configuration of both the 80 rooms and the restaurants. 'The exterior is restrained and more akin to an office building to suit its environment, so we wanted to create an internal world that opened up – almost like a briefcase – to reveal a beautiful lining and lots of quirky treasures', Norden says. 'You are invited to step away from the city and into an experience that is more textural, vibrant and exciting.'

The ground floor is designed as a series of spaces that flow into one another – from a private and tucked-away reception area to the bar and restaurant facing the street. South Place Chop House on the ground floor is a social eatery and very much intended as a local venue, with a gutsy feel and a hearty menu. The aesthetic of the Michelin-starred Angler Restaurant on the top floor is completely different, providing an atmospheric and bright space that opens up to the views of the skyline. The Angler Terrace, alongside, has an inviting rooftop garden, which comes into its own during the summer months.

The design of the guest rooms – from the standard rooms to a fantastic suite – also needed to respond to a well-travelled, well-informed business audience, with visitors coming in from many different parts of the world. The style chosen is luxurious and comfortable, with an elegant palette of materials overlaid with unique and colourful furniture and art. The provision of amenities to an opulent level was vital, with spacious bathrooms, integrated bars and substantial desks. Feature lighting here and in the communal areas became an important motif, adding drama and character.

'From the beginning there was an idea that this project should involve working with artists who had trained in London or who live in the city, so we collaborated with two young galleries that helped procure the art for the hotel', Norden says. 'Much of the artwork and lighting are bespoke, having been commissioned especially for South Place Hotel. It was all about creating something unique but keeping the setting and the audience in mind.'

'We wanted to create an internal world that opened up – almost like a briefcase – to reveal a beautiful lining and lots of quirky treasures.'
– Tina Norden

QO
Amsterdam

As an issue of growing global importance, sustainability has become a particular priority within the world of hotel design. Both major hotel groups and smaller, boutique retreats are taking environmental concerns very seriously, encouraged and supported by well-travelled and well-informed guests. Rather than simply paying lip service to sustainability, hoteliers are increasingly looking at threading green principles through the entire design and logistical paradigm of their buildings.

The QO Hotel in Amsterdam is a key example of this new approach to sustainability within the hotel industry. Instigated by Borealis Hotel Group and entrepreneur Xander Bueno de Mesquita, the QO is operated as part of the InterContinental Hotels Group, which encompasses a range of global brands, although this project is not assigned to any. As a result, it offered the opportunity to experiment with an innovative conceptual approach that takes sustainable living to a new level. 'It was a very exciting white label project to work on because it's such an ambitious project in terms of combining scale, with 300-plus rooms, and an environmentally friendly approach to everything involved with designing, building and running a hotel', says Tina Norden. 'The idea is a "circular design" and how you make the most of resources and then recycle and reuse them as best as you can. It's where you have a system – or a building – where not much energy needs to go in and very little energy comes out, so it's moving in the direction of self-sufficiency.'

The project itself, on the banks of the Amstel just outside of central Amsterdam, embraced a collaborative approach among a team of architects and designers. Architectural practices Mulderblauw and Paul de Ruiter worked on the design of the new hotel tower, using recycled and natural materials as far as possible, along with an intelligent façade that uses passive design principles to regulate the internal temperature within the highly insulated structure. Conran and Partners designed the guest-room floors, with Dutch practice Tank responsible for the public areas. 'You can see the whole building as a kind of ecosystem, with a greenhouse on the top and underground energy storage below, using warm water in a thermal aquifer', Norden says. 'It's something very special in the hotel world and also a highly creative project, so our work on the design of the bedrooms and bathrooms fits into that picture.'

Within the design of the guest rooms natural materials were used almost exclusively, with oak floors and joinery, as well as tactile elements including leather and brass. The choice of Dutch-engineered brick in the bathrooms and a Belgian limestone for the vanity units emphasises a focus on locality. Each room features full-height windows with fantastic urban views. Maximising the sense of space and the views was a priority from the outset, so Conran and Partners developed a fluid layout that allows the bedroom and bathroom to read as one space, subtly differentiated by shifts in materials and finishes. Upon entering each room, one's eye is drawn towards the vista, whilst bespoke window seats reinforce the relationship between inside and out.

'The design overall is unashamedly contemporary and clean, with careful attention to materials and detailing', says Norden. 'There's natural texture and tactility that comes from using materials in their original form and, combined with a sense of space and the quality of the finishes, it helps to encapsulate a definition of luxury within the QO brand.'

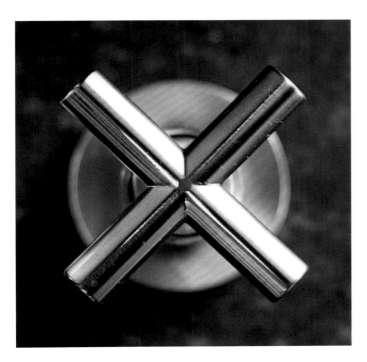

'You can see the whole building as a kind of ecosystem, with a greenhouse on the
 top and underground energy storage below.'
— Tina Norden

Maximilian
Prague

Maximilian, one of Prague's best-established boutique hotels, is situated on Haštalská Street – close to Prague's Old Town Square – and opened in 1995. The interiors were previously renovated in 2005 to a design by Czech architect Eva Jiřičná. Conran and Partners' subsequent refurbishment covers 71 guest rooms, plus the reconfiguration of existing ground-floor areas to create new public spaces including a café and bar, brasserie, library and event space with courtyard garden, alongside a full renovation of the existing basement spa.

Maximilian is owned by the Ploberger brothers, who also own the Hotel Josef in Prague. They wanted the refurbishment to contrast Josef's starker, iconic style with the softer, colourful, more playful style of Maximilian.

'Maximilian presented us with interesting challenges', says Tina Norden. 'It consists of two buildings with different architectural styles, which are connected on the ground floor by a linear series of previously underutilised public areas. Our challenge was to open up and unify these spaces to create a coherent and engaging journey for guests and visitors.'

Previously, only a limited food and beverage offer existed in the front-of-house areas. The redesign has seen the addition of a café and bar at the main entrance, which animates the building's façade and engages with the adjacent streetscape, including a small tree-lined paved area directly in front of the Haštal Church opposite. In addition, the ground-floor spaces were reworked to include a brasserie within a new living-room hub at the heart of the hotel, providing social spaces for guests and visitors.

The design approach for the hotel reflects the cultural and architectural heritage of the urban context, referencing Czech modernism and the progressive art movement influenced by famous avant-garde artist and architectural writer, Karel Teige. Teige developed a version of the modernist principle that was based on much softer elements than many of his peers, embracing texture and colour, as well as more playful elements also represented in his many surreal collage works. A strong aspect of this poetic modernism has been retained, while creating a sense of place rooted in the city and the neighbourhood. This involved drawing upon the iconic colour palette of Prague's architecture and local crafts – including weaving and glass-making – for the materiality of the design.

Bold use of colour is the defining element of the design approach. Each area of the hotel is highlighted, ranging from light green tones on entry, to pinks in the historic stairwells and a deep blue for the guest rooms. Overlaid are elements of local craft, made bespoke for the hotel, and a carefully curated selection of contemporary and classic furniture pieces in similar soft and colourful shades.

The design approach incorporates quirky guest rooms with curved ceilings within the roof space to give them a contemporary yet warm residential feel. 'We have created an approach which is playful, provocative but also functional', says Norden.

Colour features very strongly in the rooms as well, combining a deep blue with softer highlights and warm oak joinery, textured glass, mirror and brass details. The bespoke headboards reference the local craft of basket weaving, while the artwork celebrates the Czech avant-garde movement, including photomontages by Karel Teige. Each room has a window bench seat – some looking out onto the church opposite – to offer guests a direct connection with the city.

Norden adds, 'our aim was to redefine Maximilian with a clear and compelling personality which is grounded in the local context and re-establish it as a prime design destination hotel for Prague.'

The KEF Music Gallery is indicative of an important shift in the retail world from the idea of a shop to an experiential brand showcase. Within this sector, there is a growing realisation that traditional stores need to evolve rapidly in the context of digital shopping and fast-track home delivery.

Originally founded in the UK in the early 1960s, KEF is now a progressive and international company which combines innovative design and technology. The company turned to Conran and Partners to help pioneer a new retail concept to showcase the brand's sound and style.

The design of KEF's Music Gallery in Hong Kong takes inspiration from the idea of a welcoming clubhouse. The entrance sets the tone, with its use of crafted and luxurious materials, such as Atlantic stone, brass and walnut for the joinery. This part of the gallery includes a coffee bar and also a listening station for sampling headphones and smaller products. A fantastic selection of vintage modernist furniture combined with contemporary pieces sets the scene and art features prominently on the walls throughout, including pieces by Julian Opie and Yayoi Kusama from the collection of the client. 'The brief was very much about creating something that felt like a private members' club or an upscale lounge rather than a hi-fi showroom', says Tina Norden. 'But at the same time, we also needed to create a technically perfect acoustic setting and listening environment that looks effortless, so much of the layout was based on that challenge.'

At the heart of the music gallery the practice created a central listening room with the inviting atmosphere of a comfortable library. Here, bespoke joinery adds warmth and texture while the bookcases and books play a key role in the acoustic make-up of the space. There is a choice of inviting sofas and armchairs, while sliding pocket doors can be drawn across to help control the acoustic experience more fully. 'If you sit down on the sofa, you should have the perfect conditions for listening to music', Norden says. 'We gave a lot of thought in our design approach to the proportions and the materials, as well as the integration of KEF's technology into this library. The aim was to create the perfect conditions without it being at all visible to guests experiencing the space.'

The gallery as a whole offers a gentle introduction to the brand and its products, in the context of providing a respite and sanctuary within the urban fabric of Hong Kong's Central district. This soft sell will, ideally, be followed by commitment from buyers either in person or online but is based on creating brand awareness and affinity. 'It's a different and more thoughtful approach to retail than is often the case with projects of this type and on this scale', Norden says. 'We are offering an introduction to the brand and its ethos, as well as showcasing the products. Obviously, the products are for sale but, in a way, it doesn't matter so much whether your guests buy directly in store or if they go home and follow up online. What is important is ensuring that customers' initial experiences are positive and memorable.'

'The brief was very much about creating something that felt like a private members' club or an upscale lounge rather than a hi-fi showroom.'
– Tina Norden

Park Hyatt Hotels
Auckland and Jakarta

Of the range of hotel brands under the Hyatt umbrella, Park Hyatt is the most luxurious and contemporary. Its hotels are defined by individuality and character, with an emphasis on spacious guest bedrooms and suites inspired by residential architecture, as well as offering elegant dining and public spaces and wellness facilities. The design of each Park Hyatt is a bespoke response to a particular context, drawing on the local setting and surroundings.

The Park Hyatt Auckland sits in the Wynyard Quarter of the city – a harbour-front area which has recently been reinvented to create a vibrant new community adjacent to the city centre. This dedicated, seven-storey building (designed by ar+d and Bossley Architects) draws upon the Māori heritage of the region with a layered façade inspired by traditional Māori cloaks, which forms a graphic screen facing the marina. 'The hotel is on a fabulous site – right along the water's edge by the harbour, and features internal atria and expressive circular volumes', says Tina Norden. 'Within the newly regenerated area, it is really important that the ground floor should feel permeable and open to the waterfront. We've created several pedestrian routes through the building, designed to integrate closely with the surrounding public realm.'

Conran and Partners collaborated closely with the architects and also the developer – the Fu Wah International Group – on the layout of the hotel, which includes three restaurants, a spa, pool and fitness centre, and 195 guest rooms. While the ground-floor eateries and amenities seek to connect with the exterior streetscape and the marina, the spa on the first floor evokes escapism, utilising the views looking down upon the harbour.

'There are references to the water and nautical themes included in the design of the interiors', Norden says. 'But we also looked to Māori culture as a key inspiration as it is such an important part of New Zealand's heritage. We designed rugs based on Māori patterns and liaised with Māori weaver Beronia Scott to create wall panels based on decorative tukutuku woven panels typical of Māori meeting houses. Although Auckland has a sophisticated design and restaurant scene, it's not glitzy – but rather casual and organic. Therefore it was important for us to embrace that and reflect it in our approach to capture the Kiwi spirit, even in a five-star hotel.'

The practice was also asked to design the interiors of a major new Park Hyatt hotel in Jakarta (as pictured on opposite page). Set within a landmark tower – developed by MNC Land and sitting on the company media campus in the centre of the Indonesian capital – the hotel occupies the first three and the uppermost 17 floors of the 37-storey tower, with offices occupying the levels in between. Within this context, Conran and Partners was asked to design not only the interiors of the 220-plus guest rooms and suites but also the multiple food and beverage spaces, a pool, fitness centre and full-service spa, as well as a three-storey function and ballroom facility.

The triplex houses the function rooms and ballrooms at the foot of the tower, while the sky lobby on the 23rd floor has a full floor of guest spaces that include a bar, a living room and café with a dramatic staircase connecting to the main hotel restaurant and further function rooms on the floor below. The spa is arranged over two floors with a semi-outdoor pool and terraces plus a destination food and beverage complex at the very top of the tower.

The design seeks to respect Park Hyatt's guidelines while creating a luxurious sense of space for guests, drawing combined inspiration from the multicultural aspects of Jakarta and the natural beauty and traditional crafts of Indonesia. The result is contemporary but also textural, using traditional materials and vernacular references within a rich and natural palette. 'Jakarta is an Asian metropolis at the centre of a country of countless islands and an extraordinarily beautiful landscape', says Norden.

'For many people, the city is the first point of arrival in Indonesia, so we wanted to bring some of the country's natural beauty into the hotel and showcase its vast natural resources as well as Indonesian artistry and handicrafts. We have used native timbers and lots of texture from woven materials, in particular copper because it is one of the key raw materials mined in Indonesia.'

'I'm drawn to form, design and spaces that are restrained while embodying modernity and confidence', says Simon Kincaid. 'I appreciate environments which demonstrate quality, rigour and character, and designs which are executed in a clear and apparently simple way, while still having individuality and personality.'

Following a Fine Art foundation course with a focus on sculpture and three-dimensional design, Kincaid completed a degree in interior architecture at Nottingham Trent University. This degree was one of the first courses of its kind in the UK and explored how architectural principles and techniques could be applied to the insides of buildings, large and small. 'It was a well-structured course, with a real energy about it', Kincaid recalls. 'It was both vocational and creative and gave me a clear understanding of how to approach the fundamental principles relating to concept, materiality and detailing when delivering spatial designs.'

Kincaid spent his professional placement year with a London retail design and branding consultancy. At the time, its international portfolio included high-end fashion labels as well as leading high street chains, all of which had strong brand identities that needed to be understood, respected and celebrated. During this inspiring period, he learned how to switch between varying scales and typologies, a skill which is still a key aspect of his work today. 'That year helped me understand how design can be applied with customer needs, aspirations and emotions as the primary focus', Kincaid comments. 'It enabled me to appreciate what a brand stands for and how to translate and interpret that ethos within the design narrative. It also taught me how fundamental personal client relationships are to building trust, evolving brand experiences over time and, ultimately, winning new projects.'

Following graduation, Kincaid went on to work for three different London-based boutique practices, adding fresh layers of experience to his portfolio in retail, restaurant design and commercial workspaces. Moving between these complementary and interrelated sectors, Kincaid developed a valuable set of skills suited to Conran and Partners' ethos of designing for different ways of living.

Kincaid joined Conran and Partners in 2006, became a director in 2016 and a partner in 2018. His work at the practice covers various typologies including residential, hotel, restaurant and retail projects across markets ranging from the UK, Europe and North America to China, India and South Korea.

Kincaid says, 'one of the great attractions of working at Conran and Partners is that as a practice, we are deeply immersed in the creative industry, on an international level. This has allowed me to travel to culturally significant places, meet inspirational people, and enjoy experiences which have already become treasured memories. It's the culmination of these encounters, places and the people that shape them – as well as being able to work on a wide range of building typologies and across different parts of the world – that help to inspire my designs.'

Collaboration is a central element in Kincaid's approach and his projects acknowledge the importance of working closely with specialist design and brand consultants, engineers and fabricators. His contributions include the reinvention of Blake Tower in London (see page 55), a landmark brutalist building that forms part of the iconic Barbican complex in London, and the PURO Kazimierz Hotel in Kraków (see page 107), which brings together diverse visual references in a dynamic and original narrative approach. His collaborations are not only with clients – predominantly developers, entrepreneurs, operators and investors – but also with other leading architectural and design practices, both in the UK and globally.

'We tend to think in terms of complete buildings and the way in which individuals use – and relate to – our designs, irrespective of the scope of our brief', says Kincaid. 'It's a process which focuses on the quality of the journey which residents, guests or customers make through spaces, and how well-considered design can encourage personal engagement with buildings and interiors. Whichever project is currently on the drawing board is the one that interests me most, particularly when it offers an opportunity to borrow from different typologies and incorporate these into a single scheme.'

'We tend to think in terms of complete buildings and the way in which individuals use – and relate to – our designs, irrespective of the scope of our brief.'
– Simon Kincaid

PURO Kazimierz
Kraków

PURO, the Polish hotel chain, is an ambitious, progressive brand with a passion for design. This fast-growing group has opened a series of original hotels across the country in recent years, developing a lifestyle-led brand aimed at travellers looking for a sense of difference and individuality. The group asked Conran and Partners to design their flagship in the Kazimierz district of Kraków.

Kazimierz is a creative and artisanal area but also – being the old Jewish quarter – has a lot of history and an eclectic mix of period, light industrial and arts & crafts buildings.

'PURO Kazimierz has the feel of a boutique hotel but it's actually a large project with 228 guest rooms,' says Simon Kincaid. 'Our design approach was "Bohemian Modern", which represents a fusion between the energy, history, authenticity and art culture of the location and the dynamic, progressive brand principles of PURO.'

The hotel sits within a new building (designed by ASW Architekci) on the banks of the River Vistula. The design clearly references elements of the area's past, including its industrial heritage, while maintaining a strong residential feel. The design language is adapted to give each space a memorable individual identity while maintaining a cohesive flow throughout.

'The hotel features two characterful eateries – the MAK café and the Halicka restaurant – as well as lounges, a bar, an urban spa, function rooms and terraces, so there is a lot going on', says Kincaid. 'We looked very carefully at how these spaces function and flow together, despite having their own memorable and individual identities.'

This concept is carried across a collection of enticing communal and social spaces, many of which benefit from large windows and connections to adjoining outdoor spaces. There are many bespoke elements throughout, layered with colour, pattern and texture within a choice of relaxing spaces, including a library area and a sunken sitting room arranged around a central, sculptural fireplace.

The Prisma spa incorporates bold, graphic, contemporary spaces which fuse natural materials with industrial finishes and strong colours, including emerald-coloured tiles, vivid pink flooring and a saturated blue ceiling to give energy and identity.

The guest rooms and suites are lifted by a layered range of textures, including timber floors as well as vibrant tilework for the shower rooms. Space-saving design features help enhance the sense of light and volume in the smaller rooms especially, with sliding screens to separate sleeping areas and bathrooms. As Kincaid points out, 'a collaboration with local artisans and artists carries through into these urban retreats, which also feature bespoke furniture and throws, along with artworks commissioned from local artists.

'We have aimed to deliver a confident hotel with a distinctive attitude but also one which sits clearly within the PURO portfolio. It is a venue which establishes a strong connection with its locality, providing a creative and artistic environment in a social and cultural hub.'

'A fusion between the energy, history, authenticity and art culture of the location and the dynamic, progressive brand principles of PURO.'
— Simon Kincaid

Crowne Plaza
Paris

As part of a wider blueprint study for IHG, Conran and Partners undertook a significant redesign of the lobby spaces at Crowne Plaza's Paris hotel, Place de la République. The concept aims to deliver a blueprint for the definitive guest experience, while consolidating IHG's investment in the redevelopment of the Crowne Plaza brand. The former main entrance was relocated from the Place de la République along one side of the building, with access via a courtyard in the style of a traditional Parisian apartment block. The lobby – or 'plaza workspace' area – was reconfigured to meet the changing requirements of modern business travellers seeking more comfortable public and semi-public spaces in which to work and relax.

The main signature bar is now in a more prominent position closer to the outside terrace along the hotel's principal façade. Conran and Partners added The Studio, a separately bookable meeting space to cater to private meetings and events with its own bar counter and break-out lounge seating.

'Reimagining a hotel brand involves all aspects of its identity, from staff uniforms to the service strategy', says Simon Kincaid. 'Within the individual elements of a project there are always opportunities to work with manufacturers to create distinctive furniture commissions and bespoke materials. For each new development, we study the locale and create a narrative, drawing on our experience of blurring the boundaries between work and leisure to create strong, characterful places.'

The centrally located monument wall – referencing the original Haussmann-era architecture of the area – serves to orientate the guest, dividing the space between the plaza (the informal and relaxed bar spaces) and the 'galarie' (the refined and elegant reception and studio space).

Conran and Partners has also completed the design of a guest room which will serve as the basis for the wider redesign of rooms and other non-public-facing areas of the hotel, and others in the Crowne Plaza portfolio, in the future.

The Place de la République is famous as the site of the statue of Marianne – the personification of the French Republic – commemorating the founding of the First Republic of France in 1792. The hotel occupies an attractive Haussmann building, formerly a department store, with many original Haussmann features still in tact. It is located at the point where three different arrondissements (3rd, 10th and 11th) of the city meet. Conran and Partners' design also responds to the different – yet complementary – feels of each adjoining arrondissement: the 'fashionable' 3rd, 'bohemian' 10th and 'modern' 11th.

'The spaces in Place de la République are tech savvy, while acknowledging the need to embed some humanity in the design to create a comfortable place in which to work and relax', says Kincaid. 'The narrative we created for Crowne Plaza is based on the concept of "new modern". It seeks to demonstrate that business hotels can be exciting by offering guests kind, personal touches, while introducing new, meaningful experiences for them to share and – above all – to appeal to the senses as far as possible.'

The approach has also sought to reinterpret the idea of a plaza as a place where people can meet and relax and applied this to the various spaces within the hotel, encouraging guests to move between different types of space.

The design narrative has informed the choice of furniture and accessories and even the rug design and the artwork selection, which seek to reference the various key art movements and artists closely associated with Paris since the mid-nineteenth century. 'Materiality and palette are central to our design thinking. These have been used to emphasise the drama of the various spaces through effective scene-setting and a cohesive lighting strategy', says Kincaid.

This project demonstrates how leisure-orientated spaces are taking precedence over more corporate approaches to hotel design, even when they are targeted at predominantly business audiences.

'Reimagining a hotel brand involves all aspects of its identity, from staff uniforms
 to the service strategy.'
— Simon Kincaid

The Life
Seoul

Over recent years Conran and Partners has been involved in the evolution of a number of new retail concepts with a lifestyle focus. Many of these design solutions have sought to address a fast-changing global retail environment in which sales transactions are increasingly taking place online, while conventional retail stores are being transformed into showcases for products. In The Life, the focus was on a brand which sought to communicate directly with its customers and present a rounded vision of how its products might fit into their homes and daily lives.

The practice previously worked on a music gallery concept for the global hi-fi brand KEF (see page 97), and an award-winning 'omni-channel' retail hub for Marks & Spencer's 'Home' sub-brand, mixing home sets, products and advice from both staff and interactive display tools. Such innovative projects – which blur traditional boundaries between stores, experiential exhibition spaces, galleries and digital experiences – caught the attention of Emart, part of the Shinsegae retail group in South Korea. The company was looking to create a brand identity and retail environment for The Life, a new home furnishings division.

The brief was multi-layered; the flagship store concept needed to be self-contained and flexible, providing a shop within a shop that could be placed within larger Emart hypermarkets. The products themselves are seen as affordable luxuries for a well-informed but relatively young audience, particularly first-time buyers looking to furnish their new homes. The layout and aesthetic of The Life needed, therefore, to cater to this market. 'The brand design and identity – also created by Conran and Partners – uses a little bird building its nest and the strapline. "Build your home beautiful"', says Simon Kincaid. 'Our approach aimed to draw in young home-makers to big spaces offering a wide range of homeware, furniture, lighting and everything for the kitchen and bathroom. We wanted to create a journey through the store, which is an experience in itself.'

Customers are steered through the space via two clear streets and past a series of pavilions, each hosting sets of rooms which can be easily adapted according to the season. These furnished rooms offer customers inspiration and ideas, as well as placing products alongside one another in an accessible and inspiring context. Considerable thought was given to how people shop for homewares, especially furniture and big-ticket items. The combination of room sets alongside the two streets carry visitors through the store, with an open, central area offering the feel of a piazza or sunken courtyard suggesting both space and volume. The product sections, called the marketplaces, are pushed to the wings, clearly signed and logically defined to help customers navigate the store with ease. 'Seeing these pieces in situ, touching and feeling them, is important and we wanted to set that experience within a wider positive and uplifting retail environment', says Kincaid.

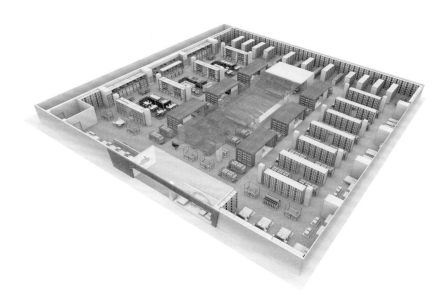

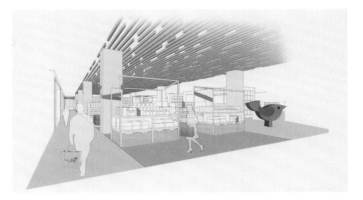

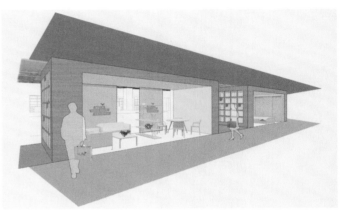

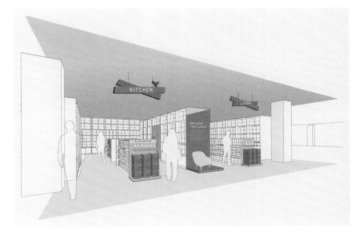

Old Bengal Warehouse
Liverpool Street, London

At one time, according to some accounts, the East India Company controlled half of the world's international trade. During the 1770s the company added to its provision of warehouses and stores with the construction of the Old Bengal Warehouse on London's New Street. The four-storey brick building was once filled with wine, spices and fabrics. Today, the Grade II-listed warehouse is home to a collection of restaurants and bars run by the D&D London restaurant and hotel group.

Conran and Partners has worked extensively with D&D, with projects including the German Gymnasium (see page 77) and the South Place Hotel (see page 83). The Old Bengal Warehouse, not far from Liverpool Street Station, offered an opportunity to create a new 'gastrodome' comparable to the practice's work on Bluebird on the King's Road or Pont de la Tour near Tower Bridge. 'There are similarities in that they are all listed buildings with very particular features and a number of different venues sitting alongside one another', says Tina Norden. 'It was a challenge to deal with a heritage building of this type and create a set of venues with their own individual characters, ensuring that they all felt – at the same time – as though they belonged together.'

The site itself offered various challenges. The configuration of the building between the ground and basement levels – with various points of entry and residential units above – steered the practice and its client towards the idea of a quartet of different spaces. Principal among these are New Street Grill and Old Bengal Bar, woven around a walled courtyard and outdoor dining areas. The aesthetic of this premium steak house reflects the history of the warehouse itself, with its exposed brick walls, broad plank wooden floors and lighting and other features with a relatively raw, masculine quality that suits the mercantile history which it evokes. The adjacent cocktail bar has memories of Indian colonial clubs with heritage panelling etched into contemporary mirror panels. 'We spent a lot of time looking not only in the spaces themselves but also delving into the story of the East India Company and its relationship with this part of London', Norden says. 'We used different parts of that storyline to inform the various spaces within the "gastrodome", so in the Grill – for example – we commissioned artwork of shipping captains but with folded newspaper hats and tongue-in-cheek, playful touches. We wanted it to feel as though it has been there for a very long time, hence the introduction of characterful old brickwork and the retention of original floors where we were able to, as well as using a lot of reclaimed materials.'

Aside from New Street Grill and Old Bengal Bar, there is also the Fish Market restaurant – which has its own terrace – and the New Street Wine Shop, the latter echoing the original purpose of the warehouse as a wine and spices store. With its own identity and branding, Fish Market is a restaurant with a distinct ethos, forming another key part of this family of spaces. It is intended to be a more casual and affordable sibling, with a seafood-oriented menu and a bright and casual feel. New Street Wine Shop completes the quartet and not only offers a fine selection of wines by the bottle and glass, but has become a favourite for an after-dinner drink in a beautiful daylit space with original brickwork and features.

The Guesthouse
Vienna

The design of The Guesthouse in Vienna, for developer JP Immobilien, offers a key example of the way in which Conran and Partners' work in the residential arena has influenced its work in the field of hospitality, and vice versa. At The Guesthouse – a member of the Design Hotels cooperative – the emphasis is upon the guest rooms and suites, which have the quality and feel of beautifully crafted and carefully curated apartments. Spacious and inviting, these are living spaces where residents can enjoy spending time.

The setting is, certainly, very special. The Guesthouse sits close to the Vienna State Opera and the Albertina Museum and is surrounded by galleries, landmark buildings and parks, all in easy walking distance. From the hotel itself, the skyline offers a mesmerising panorama, hence the provision of window seats as well as sofas and armchairs in rooms.

The crafted interiors of the rooms and suites take inspiration from the rich design history of the city itself, drawing upon the influence of both the pioneering Vienna Secession movement and Austrian mid-century designers. The level of finish and detailing is all-important, within a sophisticated urban aesthetic. Along with many bespoke elements, there is a highly curated approach to the art and furnishings, including armchairs by Friedrich Kiesler and crockery and china from Lilien Porzellan. The choice of materials throughout reflects the importance of craft and texture, with a palette of oak, brass and marble within a luxurious and comfortable setting. 'There are a lot of beautiful natural materials and joyful elements', says Tim Bowder-Ridger. 'There are classic Viennese pieces, but we also worked with local artisans, like the metalsmith Carl Auböck, which gives a unique character to the spaces. At the top of the hotel we were able to create a series of duplex spaces, with mezzanines looking down on the sitting rooms, offering variety within the rooms and suites.'

There are, in all, 39 rooms and suites, including the duplex and courtyard suites. At the heart of the building is the ground floor, designed as much as a neighbourhood destination in its own right as a hotel restaurant, which creates a strong link with the surrounding city space. It is filled – day and night – with local people who have come to regard it as a key meeting place for business and pleasure. Conran and Partners also designed an in-house brasserie and bakery, drawing inspiration from the famous coffee shops and cafés of the city. Here, the materiality and lighting design in particular are key elements within a crafted, modern approach.

The narrative has even influenced the way the hotel is run on a day-to-day basis, a guest-focused experience with a very loyal following. 'Personally, I love to sit in my room, look out of the window and engage with Vienna', says Bowder-Ridger. 'That sense of being part of the city is very important and it's what really drove our approach to the design of the interiors. In this highly urban setting, it's a very contextual project.'

Niki Club East
Nasu, Tochigi

As well as its work on many urban hotels around the world, Conran and Partners has also been involved in the creation of a number of rural retreats. These include Niki Club East in the Tochigi Prefecture of Japan. Around two hours away from Tokyo, Nasu is an area of particular beauty, famous for its hot springs, forests, mountains and ski resorts. Here, the founders of Niki Club created a retreat connected to the landscape, combining a modern ethos with a focus on well-being and locally sourced food. Beginning with just six rooms, the resort gradually expanded to include 14 hectares (34 acres) of land as well a range of amenities and guest pavilions.

Conran and Partners became involved in the expansion of Niki Club with a brief to design and build a new communal hub, as well as 24 new pavilions within the grounds. The practice was involved in the master planning of this, the third phase of Niki Club, along with both the architecture and interior architecture. 'It's a very beautiful, rural area and a real antidote to the metropolis of Tokyo', says Tim Bowder-Ridger. 'It's the kind of place where people come for a few nights to detox and there are lovely walks through the woods. In May, you can sleep with the windows open and hear the sounds of nature outside your pavilion, including a whole chorus of bull frogs singing in the nearby fields.'

The project began with careful consideration of the placement of the various new buildings in the landscape, while examining the journey of arrival and the way in which guests navigate their way through the grounds. Beyond this, each building needed to forge its own sense of connection with the surroundings. 'It's a project that sought to demonstrate an understanding of Japanese culture', Bowder-Ridger says. 'The buildings needed to become part of this environment so they are very much about the inside–outside relationship, as is the case with one of our other projects in Japan, Kita Aoyama [see page 42]. Even when you are inside, it's important to feel engaged with the landscape and that extended to the idea of fresh-air baths and outdoor rooms.'

The concrete-framed cabins feature extensive glazing, opening onto private decks and terraces looking out into the trees, while timber cladding softens their appearance. As well as single-storey pavilions, Conran and Partners also designed two-storey guesthouses with double-height living spaces and mezzanine sleeping areas. The club house features more extensive use of concrete, but its impact on the site has been carefully mitigated by tucking the building into the topography and contrasting transparency with mass. The restaurant and other amenity spaces look out across the landscape, while pools and water features around the building enhance the connection with nature. 'Using simple materials that would mellow gracefully was very important', Bowder-Ridger says. 'The timber used for the pavilions works well in this woodland setting but so does the beautifully made Japanese concrete. The landscaping around the buildings was also crucial and has matured over time, softening everything and creating a synergy between the buildings and their surroundings.'

'The landscaping around the buildings was crucial and has matured over time, softening everything and creating a synergy between the buildings and their surroundings.'
— Tim Bowder-Ridger

The Conran Shop
Seoul, South Korea

British lifestyle brand The Conran Shop was founded by Terence Conran in 1973, and soon established itself as one of the leading lifestyle retailers in the world, offering an eclectic, hand-selected collection of gifts, furniture, lighting and personal accessories from some of the world's most respected designers and emerging talents.

The Conran Shop partnered with retail conglomerate Lotte for this venture, and the Seoul store – in the city's Gangnam district – adds to a portfolio of 11 other outlets across the world.

Working closely with The Conran Shop's in-house creative team, Conran and Partners evolved the brand experience to create a high-impact, lifestyle-led retail environment that responds to the vibrant retail culture of the city.

The design approach opens up the perimeter to allow maximum light into the building, as well as optimising views in and out. Switch-back escalators in the centre of the store act as a dramatic architectural feature and encourage circulation between the two floors.

'We wanted to create what is, effectively, a contemporary gallery space which allows The Conran Shop to curate its products and encourages customers to engage with those products in an atmospheric, dramatic and stimulating retail environment', says Simon Kincaid. 'The contrast between the two floors adds a sense of theatre and surprise to the experience, as well as giving variation and depth to the product merchandising.'

The store has two distinct identities. The ground floor space is clean and light, combining concrete, steel and glass elements with fully-exposed services to create an experimental lab feel.

A product gallery of white rectilinear display plinths welcomes customers upon arrival, centring around a cast concrete sales desk. The ground floor also incorporates a prominently positioned 'Orby' café. Whilst consistent with the minimal aesthetic, the café adds a palette of cast concrete, perforated steel and timber furniture, complete with a full range of Carl Hansen dining chairs.

In contrast, the first floor – where high-quality residential furniture products are displayed – presents a richly atmospheric club feel, encouraging interaction with products at a more leisurely pace. The dark finish used for the ceiling introduces a low eyeline, with timber floors softening the acoustics, warming the ambience and adding a more luxe domestic feel. The iconic Conran Shop chair wall takes on a new form using dark terrazzo and a blackened frame and incorporating a display of 54 iconic chairs.

The two floors are united by a 'Conran Blue' core, the vibrant brand colour acting as a navigational marker for customer orientation.

Kincaid explains, 'our design creates opportunities to enjoy the experience of browsing products as much as the pleasure of purchasing them. Small experiential pockets such as a black-on-black lighting room on the first-floor, offer customers an immersive environment in which the lighting products pop like jewels in the night. We have also designed VIP rooms with walnut-panelled walls and a whisky display referencing the founder's favourite tipple, to exude the ambience of a members' club.'

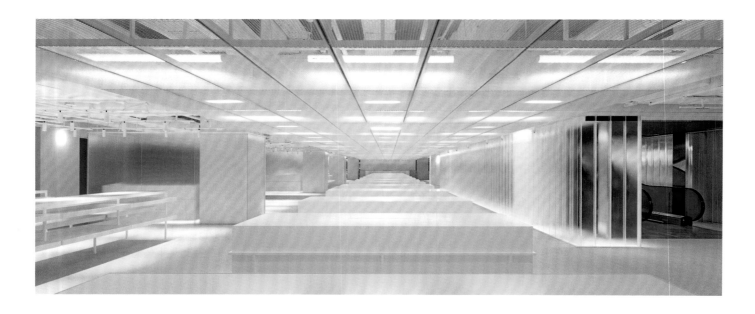

'The contrast between the two floors adds a sense of theatre and surprise to the experience, as well as giving variation and depth to the product merchandising.'
– Simon Kincaid

Place

Key to Conran and Partners' approach to architecture and design is a consideration of the spaces between buildings and the experience of the wider stakeholders adjacent to a project or those passing through it. This can involve working at a large scale to repair a neighbourhood, stitching it into a wider context, or looking at an individual building that might act as a catalyst for regenerating a neighbourhood.

From the very beginning, Conran and Partners has nurtured a particular interest in place-making in its widest sense. This preoccupation stretches back to the formative years of the practice, and since then it has designed a vast number of small and large-scale developments, master plans and mixed-use schemes, as well as a range of neighbourhood projects. Whilst high-end projects often receive a great deal of publicity, many of the practice's commissions are anchored around a blend of social housing, private homes and other ownership models. Key to the partners' ambitions is ensuring equal care and thought is given to all projects, whatever the budget.

'We have always approached regeneration and master planning projects in a way which is inherently our own', says Tim Bowder-Ridger.

The team's approach is always to consider how people occupy spaces and how they respond to them. From the start they place the person at the centre and think about how they will feel in a place or space. Only then do they start to build outwards.

At the beginning of any project the team looks at the 24-hour life cycle of a space and creates individual profiles of residents. These might be a parent, a schoolchild or a commuter heading off to work. Consideration is then given to what a typical day for each of these people might look like and how that relates to this particular place. The designers can then start to imagine patterns of lives crossing over and understand how they might come together and what we can do to make that daily experience a little better. It is as if we are creating a particular journey for everyone using and affected by the project.

This people-centric approach applies to a wide range of community projects. Some of these are – relatively speaking – quite modest in scale, such as the restoration and revival of Saltdean Lido in Brighton and Hove as a well-loved neighbourhood landmark and amenity. The practice has also designed a new public piazza as part of a mixed-use project at Lower Marsh, in London's Waterloo district, home to a vibrant and engaged community (see page 171).

Even a single, modest-scale building can have a catalytic effect on a whole neighbourhood. For instance, for some years after completion it was recognised that the Boundary redevelopment (see page 163) had been one of the new

1. Saltdean Lido, Brighton, photographed in 1938 **2.** Futako Tamagawa, Tokyo

projects that had triggered a wider regeneration around Shoreditch High Street in East London. This was achieved by giving particular attention to the way the building engages with the street. Having a local café in place of an exclusive hotel reception is something that has subsequently become more common, not least due to Ace Hotel's drive in this direction. But we are now seeing this increasingly occurring in commercial buildings too, such as in the practice's intervention in 200 Gray's Inn Road, London (see page 166), where the ground-level spaces are positively contributing to the street and public realm at an incremental level, reversing the decades of dehumanising our streets.

Over time the practice has also been increasingly involved in large-scale projects in the UK and Asia. These include Portobello Square in London, which encompasses hundreds of homes – and thousands of residents – within an ambitious regeneration project; and Futako Tamagawa in Tokyo (see page 139), a 23-hectare mixed-use quarter with a strong residential component and an emphasis on communal green space for the district as a whole. At the time of construction this was also Tokyo's largest single project.

As with all Conran and Partners' schemes, even at the largest scale there is an emphasis on identity. Similar to other project types, the research process undertaken at the start of each commission encompasses a close examination of the cultural, historical and social context that helps generate the unique character and provenance of a neighbourhood, while always remembering to place the residents at the heart of this context. The difference, however, is that this consideration may need to be expanded to the wider neighbourhood or district. In part, this is achieved through extensive consultations with stakeholders with an aim to give them greater ownership of the project.

In the Green Man Lane project (see page 156), in the London borough of Ealing, for instance, incorporating a local primary school became a vital part of this process, carrying the sense of identity forward while improving an all-important amenity for the community. Supporting this, community cafés, allotments, play parks and garden squares were incorporated to form part of the social adhesion that binds neighbourhoods together.

The evolution of rounded, diverse and engaging communities and neighbourhoods also involves the successful integration of many other amenities, from schools and nurseries, to retail and restaurants, as well as parks, piazzas and outdoor spaces. As a collaborative practice with experience in many types of projects, Conran and Partners is in a strong position to create a cohesive community with a particular sense of place.

3. Concept sketch of Portobello Square, London **4.** Albion Café, Shoreditch, London

Futako Tamagawa
Tokyo, Japan

Conran and Partners has been working in Japan for over 25 years. Projects include resort hotels, such as the Niki Club East (see page 127) and smaller high-end residential projects, such as a significant residential building for NTT Urban Development in Kita Aoyama, Tokyo (see page 42). The most ambitious of these projects, certainly in terms of scale, is Futako Tamagawa, also in Tokyo, which extends over 20 hectares (nearly 50 acres), and offers some 400,000 sq m of office, leisure, retail and residential floor space, making it one of the largest developments in the city in recent years.

The practice won a limited competition for Futako Tamagawa, an urban quarter that sits alongside the banks of the Tama River in the Setagaya district of Tokyo. The river here is broad and features long strips of parkland and open spaces along its banks; as such, the Tama forms a green lung stretching through the metropolis. As master planners and design architects for this 13-year, mixed-use project, Conran and Partners prioritised the importance of landscaping and open communal spaces, further enhancing the fresh, open character of the riverside.

'It's quite a dense residential district overall and we wanted to create a green stepping stone of scale that carries you through to the River Tama', says Tim Bowder-Ridger. 'We designed a new green landscape which envelopes a series of generous retail spaces. This provides a much-used amenity for the whole neighbourhood, not just for residents of the estate, many of whom live in a number of tall towers that form part of the master plan.'

The emphasis on green space within this process of place-making led to a close collaboration with landscape designers Landscape Plus Inc and the broader team of local architects and consultants. The project was split into two phases and includes not only the new amenity spaces but also department stores, a retail galleria, an office building, three residential towers and two additional low-rise residential buildings. Futako Tamagawa also connects with the local train station, served by two arterial lines.

The design incorporates a circulation ribbon which cuts through the new landscape populated by retail between the railway and the far end of the public park. Working with the landscape designer, the practice created a series of ponds and rivulets as well as the green spaces themselves. Residents and visitors to the development are able to enjoy these outdoor park areas.

Futako Tamagawa has won awards for both its residential quarter and its landscaping. As such, it is comparable with major projects in other cities, such as Walthamstow Stadium (see page 22) and Green Man Lane (see page 156), both in London, where garden squares, play zones and communal and private open-air spaces are vital ingredients of the master planning and essential components of community itself. It also adopts a similar green stepping stone approach to another Conran and Partners and Landscape Plus Inc collaboration for Kita Aoyama, which incorporates a series of generous landscaped terraces in natural stone.

Place   Futako Tamagawa, Tokyo, Japan

'We designed a new green landscape which envelopes a series of generous
retail spaces. This provides a much-used amenity for the whole neighbourhood,
not just for residents of the estate, many of whom live in a number of tall towers
that form part of the master plan.'
– Tim Bowder-Ridger

Butler's Wharf
Tower Bridge, London

A project of great scale, imagination and ambition, and the first large-scale project for the practice in London (under its previous name Conran Roche), Butler's Wharf provides an important exemplar of riverside regeneration. It is also an early example of the practice reinventing existing buildings and neighbourhoods, layering in new purposes and new constructions amongst the existing ones to retain the memories of the location whilst creating a relevance for the present and the future.

This 4.5-hectare site blends the conversion of historic warehouses with new buildings, while offering a mixture of residential apartments, office space, restaurants, shops and cultural amenities. Today, a generation later, it remains a thriving community and a highly desirable location on the banks of the River Thames, sitting alongside Tower Bridge, forming part of a fully regenerated waterfront that continues east and west.

This project was very much one of the pioneering regeneration projects of the early post-industrial Margaret Thatcher era via the London Docklands Development Corporation. The original site, which was owned by P&O, was run down and partially derelict. Some of the Victorian warehouses were still serving as stores for spices and other uses, while others were occupied by artists, who turned the large and open spaces into studios. Terence Conran, who first glimpsed the site and its potential on a summer party boat trip down the river, proposed a mixed-use approach, which would include focal-point destinations. Chief among these were the original Design Museum, a highly ambitious and demanding project in itself, and a series of waterfront restaurants, including Le Pont de la Tour, a gastrodome which incorporates two restaurants, a delicatessen and a wine shop.

The Butler's Wharf project spanned a decade, beginning with the master plan and progressing in stages. A number of warehouses, including the pivotal Butler's Wharf building itself, were restored, with retail and restaurants at ground level and apartments above. This conversion process was, on its own, challenging, particularly given that the foundations of the Butler's Wharf building were minimal, and the original structure needed to be rebuilt using a new internal concrete framework. A number of new buildings, including student residences and offices, many of which were designed by the practice, were included, which added to the overall diversity and character of the project. Terence Conran himself chose to live in the new neighbourhood for many years above Conran and Partners' former London studio.

"The scale and complexity of Butler's Wharf is comparable to some of our later projects such as Green Man Lane in West London (see page 156), and Futako Tamagawa in Tokyo (see page 139), and very much influenced our approach to their design', says Tim Bowder-Ridger. 'Butler's Wharf was the first of our major regeneration schemes and rapidly became a model for other mixed-use developments in terms of understanding how to create new neighbourhoods in distinctive contexts and sustainable communities.'

'At the time, people said nobody would cross the river to the wharf but, of course,
 they were completely wrong.'
– Tim Bowder-Ridger

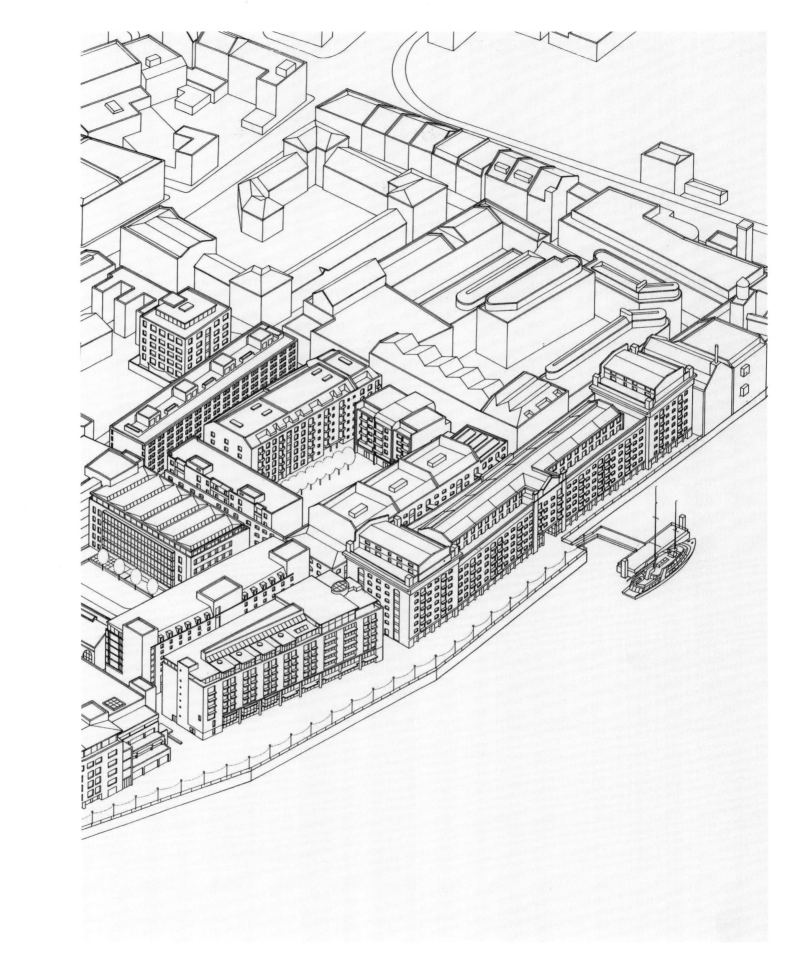

Architect Malcolm Parry, former Head of the Welsh School of Architecture and a passionate modernist, was one of the most formative influences on Lee Davies while a student in Cardiff. Parry was something of a celebrity, presenting a number of architectural programmes on television and radio, with a strong belief that good architecture should be accessible and could make a real difference – not just to the built environment but to people's daily lives. 'Malcolm Parry is a highly charismatic Welshman: enthusiastic, dynamic and flamboyant', says Davies.

'His enthusiasm for architecture was infectious. I recall our first-year study trip to the Netherlands, where his explanation of the modernist buildings made a huge impression on me. Malcolm provided such a deep understanding of what architecture was all about, focusing on issues such as a building's orientation and the importance of daylight – early lessons that have stayed with me throughout my career.'

One of the memorable buildings Davies experienced as a student was Michel de Klerk's Het Schip in Amsterdam, a housing association project built on socialist principles. 'It was aimed at workers but was about creating a beautiful environment for them to live in', says Davies. 'The approach sought to offer an opportunity of a better life through good design to those who experienced little beauty during their working days. It provided them with something that could be appreciated and enjoyed when they came home.' Another influential scheme which Davies visited during the same trip was Hilversum Town Hall by Willem Dudok. This offered a compelling insight into how a single architect can work holistically across a scheme, achieving a strong balance between form and function and designing everything from the overall site concept to the ironmongery and finishes of the building.

Davies grew up near Cardiff, a period during which he developed a particular passion for creating, drawing and painting. Artistic influences in his family were strong – his mother was a seamstress and his father a potter, artist and teacher – and they were ultimately major influences in his ambition to become an architect.

Following graduation, Davies initially moved to London, where he worked on a range of residential and regeneration schemes with several different architectural practices. This included some time with the project architects for Montevetro, an apartment building by the River Thames designed by Richard Rogers Partnership. Soon after joining Conran and Partners, Davies recalls how Terence Conran – who owns an apartment in Montevetro – discovered Davies' connection with the building and invited him to his home. 'It was quite a special moment for me', Davies reflects, 'talking to Terence and his family about the design, hearing about how much they enjoyed living there and seeing how well it had endured the test of time.'

Before joining Conran and Partners, Davies had decided to relocate to Brighton to start a family. There he established the practice's second UK studio. Among his key projects is Baylis Old School in Lambeth, South London (see page 151), which involved the reinvention of a group of listed 1960s buildings on the site, as well as creating new homes and amenities within the former school campus. The approach combined elements of master planning and place-making, as well as restoration and retrofitting. Davies is currently leading the regeneration of the Green Man Lane area of Ealing (see page 156), West London. This project – the practice's largest single built scheme in the UK since Butler's Wharf (see page 142) – has involved engaging and working with residents and keeping the existing community together, listening to their needs and ambitions and reinventing the original estate. 'We continually strive to create designs that meet society's needs, while still being beautiful pieces of architecture. Working with existing communities and embarking on a creative journey together is a complex but highly rewarding process', says Davies, 'and key to finding the best way forward with residents is to listen, understand and to develop a strong affinity with them.'

This dynamic approach has also seen the introduction of a range of new buildings to the Green Man Lane estate, including townhouses, apartments and a new school. It represents a layered and imaginative regeneration scheme – with a rich, integrated mix of tenures and typologies – an approach which Davies shares with all the partners. His work places a clear emphasis on the connection between a specific project and its wider neighbourhood. Each is a community with its own distinctive identity, requiring a bespoke solution suited to that particular area and site. It recognises the unique quality inherent in every project and ensures this is reflected in all aspects of the delivery of every development.

'We continually strive to create designs that can meet society's needs, while still being beautiful pieces of architecture.'
– Lee Davies

Baylis Old School
Lambeth, London

During the 1960s, the London County Council commissioned a series of new comprehensive schools across the capital. One of the most accomplished of these was the Lilian Baylis School in Lambeth, named in honour of the theatre producer Lilian Mary Baylis, who once ran The Old Vic and Sadler's Wells. The school, designed as a modern campus, consisted of a series of modest buildings arranged around courtyards and playgrounds. When it eventually moved to a new setting, the old site – which is Grade II listed – became available for redevelopment following a long period of neglect. Conran and Partners was invited – as architects – by Henley Homes to reinvent the old campus based on a sustainable vision, working with the existing buildings while also adding new-build elements to create a total of 149 homes. These range from one-bedroom apartments to family townhouses. In doing so, the derelict old school was saved and transformed into a vibrant new community.

'Our clients saw that the Old School had a characteristic charm and style that could give the project a unique identity and presence', says Lee Davies.

Following a design competition, Conran and Partners was appointed to realise the potential of this project. They began by getting to know the historic buildings and were fortunate to meet the original architect, Bob Sealy from the Architects Co-Partnership (ACP). Bob provided the design team with invaluable insight into the thinking behind the design and responded positively to the conversion proposals. ACP gave the team access to its drawing archives and original design strategies, assisting Conran and Partners to form an understanding of the essence of the original building design. As a result, a new reflecting water pool was introduced to the main courtyard area, something which had been proposed within the original 1960s master plan.

The practice was able to draw on its expertise of working with heritage buildings and engaging with existing communities while reinventing the former school as a residential development which is outward-looking and offers a new approach to living in the 21st century.

The team wanted to preserve what was there and reuse it, to build on the unique identity of the expressed concrete structure, expansive brickwork and generous runs of glazing with linked blocks, while adding some subtle new extensions.

'We converted the existing classroom blocks into apartments. These are not unlike a set of stacked drawers pulled partly open so they project out, one on top of another. The concrete and brick, rather than being austere, have a softness. The original generous-sized windows have been retained and restored, flooding the living spaces with natural daylight', says Davies.

The apartments within the old classrooms and library look over a series of asymmetrical garden squares and communal courtyards, which include planting and water features. These help define the special character of the project as a whole, while enhancing the experiential quality of daily living at the Baylis Old School, along with integrated play areas for families.

As well as the more modest extensions, the site also offered sufficient space to create some substantial new additions, with a combination of brick-faced townhouses and apartments in a U-shaped formation connecting with both the surrounding streetscape and broader neighbourhood, as well as providing additional communal gardens to the rear.

'The new buildings take inspiration from the spirit and nature of the original school', says Davies, 'and the brick, especially, helps to tie together the new and the old, reinforcing a sense of identity and place. These elements also gave us the opportunity to create a new garden square, which links to the reimagined historic courtyards, an important part of the project as a whole. This project is just as much about the spaces which the buildings create as the buildings themselves.'

One of the great things about the project is the sense of variety it encapsulates. Within the conversion, nothing is standard or repeatable, so each apartment is inherently unique with bespoke characteristics. A once derelict set of buildings has been transformed into a vibrant and unique new community, creating a bespoke development that draws on its rich history and secures its long-term future for this important set of buildings and the courtyard spaces they create.

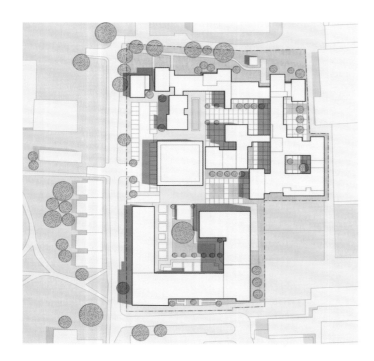

'These are not unlike a set of stacked drawers pulled partly open so they project
 out, one on top of another.'
– Lee Davies

Green Man Lane and St John's Primary School
Ealing, London

The transformation of the Green Man Lane estate in Ealing, West London, is an ambitious and multilayered project designed to repair and reconnect a run-down neighbourhood and enhance the daily lives of existing residents. The original estate dates back to the early 1970s when it had a strong and vibrant community. However, it suffered from poor-quality building stock which had led to a number of wider social concerns. Conran and Partners was appointed as master planners and project architects – in conjunction with housing provider A2Dominion and construction company Rydon – to work with local people to shape new plans for the area, creating around 770 new homes, complementary communal amenities and an array of public and private open spaces, as well as a new primary school.

This complex, multiphased regeneration project – spread over more than 15 years – has involved the gradual replacement of original parts of the estate, while continuing to keep the existing community together. Davies says, 'the process involved extensive consultation with the wider community over a long period of time, empowering local participation in the evolution of the design, while building trust that is central to a truly people-centric approach.' The new buildings include apartment blocks of up to eight storeys, as well as terraced brick townhouses that combine modern aesthetics with a familiar local material and typology. The mix of homes ranges from one-bedroom flats to four-bedroom apartments and houses.

Within the master plan there are communal gardens and parks, retained mature trees supplemented with substantial tree planting, as well as plazas and other public spaces. Each house and apartment has generous windows and its own private outdoor space, whether a private garden, a terrace or a balcony. Importantly, the first phase included a dramatic cyma-curved frontage building that incorporates a community café and energy centre.

A new primary school now serves as the focal point for the Green Man Lane project and was the result of a collaborative approach between Ealing Council's housing and education departments, the development team and Conran and Partners. To realise this opportunity to create a heart for the community, the team proposed a land swap that saw the existing school (also dating from the 1970s) remain open while the new one was constructed and prepared for staff and pupils to move into. The site area of the existing school was reconfigured to free up land for additional homes, the sale of which has helped to fund the construction of the school.

The architectural design itself creates a strong street form and conveys a mature learning environment while giving the new school a distinct identity. The design approach beyond the façade follows a more domestic narrative that blends familiarity and innovation to encourage an active and comfortable learning environment. It combines traditional materials and forms – such as the twin pitched roof used for the brick-clad school building – with many fresh concepts, including a roof terrace, pop-out windows and a sculptural copper façade. Natural materials have been selected throughout, from pre-oxidised copper to weathered buff brick, providing robustness that will stand the test of time as well as tactile warmth. The new school has provided sufficient space to allow for future expansion of pupil numbers, whilst the plan of the building helps to shelter hidden playgrounds at ground and rooftop levels as well as create garden spaces for outdoor play and learning.

'There's a lot of communal pride associated with the scheme, which demonstrates how, by building high levels of trust, a holistic approach to neighbourhood planning can result in the delivery of successful, integrated and safer neighbourhoods', says Lee Davies.

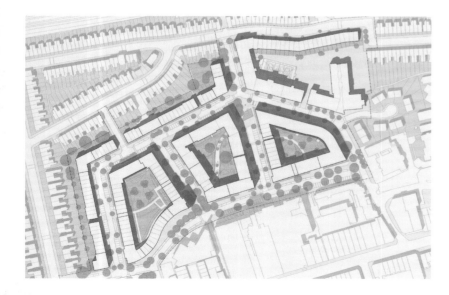

'The process involved extensive consultation with the wider community over a long period of time, empowering local participation in the evolution of the design, while building trust that is central to a truly people-centric approach.'
– Lee Davies

York Road
Maidenhead

York Road is a strategic town centre site in Maidenhead, approximately 50 km (30 miles) to the west of London. As master planners and architects, Conran and Partners has designed a scheme in the city which seeks to establish an open campus feel around new landscaping and a library square by creating a cultural and residential quarter with 229 homes, 88 of which will be affordable. As well as providing an enhanced setting for the existing town hall and Grade II-listed library with public spaces, restaurants and cafés, the design will also increase connectivity within the city centre. 'This site played to our strength of designing within a historic context', says Victoria Whenray.

Architecturally, the scheme draws on the existing, rich patina of red brick and the rigour demonstrated in the local heritage: the legacy of the Victorian industrial age – including some of Brunel's celebrated engineering projects – and the library which forms one of the site edges. By formulating a clear understanding of the context, the practice was able to create a distinct sense of place that was fitting to the character of this key area of Maidenhead, enabling the delivery of a vital new neighbourhood for people to live, work and socialise.

Clustered, tall elements create wayfinding markers which point towards the waterway, whilst low-scale townhouses sit alongside existing Victorian buildings at the site fringes. A series of linked urban squares lead to a waterside promenade, incorporating accessible, legible, active and sustainable design. Clear visual corridors celebrating the listed library as the centrepiece of this new urban campus preserve views of the distinctive building from the town centre. The master plan sensitively integrates with the overall town centre context by retaining existing street patterns and adding moments of height to signify the east–west connection to York Stream via a generous new public square. This square is bounded on three sides by the library, town hall and waterway. Retail and other commercial activities will occupy the ground-floor areas along the fourth side.

Conran and Partners' design response has been to present elevations with a certain gravitas around the town hall square through the careful use of materiality and texture. The ground floors in particular are designed as strong, almost imposing, elements. The upper parts of the buildings have a lighter touch with large expanses of glazing, balconies and shared raised gardens, mediating between public and private. The project completes the civic heart of Maidenhead: creating a journey between the very public new heart of the town centre and the privacy of people's homes was an integral part of the design narrative.

The design delivers much-needed homes for local people whilst creating a new neighbourhood in the town centre with a mixture of residential, retail and museum facilities. Improving access to the natural waterway, York Stream, as well as retaining a large number of mature trees, forms an essential part of the landscaping strategy, influencing the positioning and scale of the new buildings. 'We have endeavoured to create a neighbourhood which is embedded in a sense of place and in the hope that people will develop an emotional connection with it over time', says Whenray.

The site is within five minutes' walk from Maidenhead Station and will be served by the newly constructed, cross-London Elizabeth Line. Whenray says, 'we have taken a relatively run-down part of the town – previously occupied by temporary car parking on the site of a demolished 1960s office building – and transformed it into a highly attractive, functioning part of the urban environment.'

York Road is part of a wider regeneration proposal from the Maidenhead Development Partnership – a joint venture between the Royal Borough of Windsor and Maidenhead and Countryside Properties – to redevelop four council-owned sites in the town centre, covering more than six hectares. The overall regeneration will transform the centre of Maidenhead over the next decade and provide an additional 1,200 homes when complete.

Boundary
Shoreditch, London

Situated in a thriving quarter of Shoreditch, Boundary represented a fresh collaboration with Terence Conran. Together with his business partners Vicki Conran and Peter Prescott, Terence acquired a former printworks on a relatively open corner site. Here, Conran and Prescott developed ideas for a multilayered project (somewhat reminiscent of past successes such as Bluebird on the King's Road) and asked Conran and Partners to work on the design for this new lifestyle concept.

The building was converted and updated but also extended upwards. There is a distinction between the brick of the original Victorian printworks and the copper-clad addition and roof terrace above it. 'While there's a definite contrast, and a clear difference between old and new, importantly, the two work naturally together', says Tim Bowder-Ridger.

On the ground floor of the Boundary building, the practice designed Albion – an informal but elegant café, bar and grocery store that is open all day long, every day of the week. Understated and crafted, Albion features a palette dominated by timber floors and joinery, exposed brick and semi-industrial lighting, while making the most of the big windows and views of the streetscape. 'At street level, Albion really connects with the neighbourhood. It attracts locals who drop in with their laptops for a coffee or to pick something up from the grocery store', Bowder-Ridger says. Below this at basement level a high-

end French style restaurant in a classic Terence Conran vein was added and is frequented by business people from the nearby financial district. Interestingly, in this highly urban context, the rooftop bar and grill appeals to both audiences, offering both a heated orangery and an outdoor terrace for the warmer months. Looking out across the London skyline, this rooftop retreat with its secret garden has an escapist quality.

'The Boundary includes a collection of hotel rooms and suites and conceptually was about creating restaurants with rooms rather than the other way around as is traditional in the mainstream market. Some of these were designed by Terence and Vicki Conran, whilst others were conceived by guest designers such as Sir David Tang or took inspiration from Terence's 20th-century design heroes. There is, therefore, a distinctive character to each one, each catering to different tastes and predilections. Regular guests often try out a variety of rooms before gravitating towards their favourite, to which they invariably return on future visits', says Bowder-Ridger.

Combining these various different elements has created a vibrant micro-community within the building, as well as an important local amenity. Boundary has played a part in the successful regeneration story of Shoreditch as a whole, which has become – over time – one of the most creative and eclectic of London's many villages.

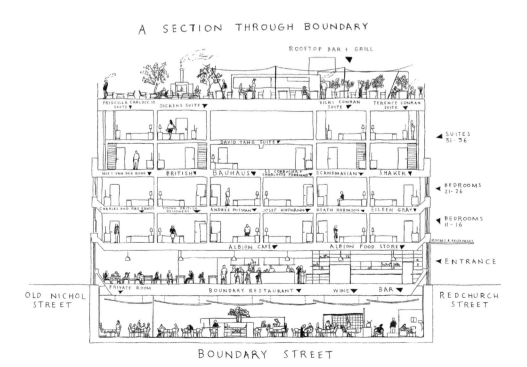

'Looking out across the London skyline, this rooftop retreat with its secret garden
has an escapist quality.'
— Tim Bowder-Ridger

200 Gray's Inn Road
Central London

Great Portland Estates plc (GPE) commissioned Conran and Partners to redesign the ground floor of one of London's most prominent office buildings, 200 Gray's Inn Road. Originally designed by Foster + Partners in 1991, the building is occupied by several high-profile media organisations, including ITN Productions, ITV and Warner Bros. GPE felt that the conventionally configured office reception was no longer fit for purpose and sought to adapt the space to respond to the changing work culture of modern occupiers; one which blurs the edges between work and leisure time. As a result, a new approach was required to respond to changing user expectations, the on-demand culture and growing competition from the maturing and agile co-working, short-lease sector.

The updated design of the reception area exudes the feel of a private members' club, blended with café culture and a hotel experience all within a single space. The new ground floor has transformed the arrival experience and provided a much-needed amenity, changing the way occupiers and visitors use the building. 'The building's original architecture uses materials which are simple but robust, predominantly concrete, granite, aluminium and glass', says Simon Kincaid.

Equally authentic materials have been included to warm and soften areas of the ground floor, including terrazzo, metal, timber and leather. In some places, the design creates new interventions. For example, lighting elements are installed within the existing structural concrete coffers to complement the inherent design features of the building, while oak panels and partitions give a warm, natural and soft feeling to the ground-floor area. The design serves to provide a stronger connection between the external, urban environment and the building's interior at street level, breaking down the barrier between the public and corporate environments and drawing people into the space.

Conran and Partners' redesign utilises the generous width of the façade along Gray's Inn Road. It creates a subtle – yet crucial – division in the way the 2,000 or more people based in the building and their guests are able to flow through the lobby while still allowing them to be drawn into the café and lounge areas. The approach creates pockets of space: lounge seating, booths and sharing tables, to encourage users to occupy differing areas within the same space.

Key features include a bespoke reception desk designed in terrazzo, and a co-working table to encourage staff to use the space as an extension of their offices. Conran and Partners worked in collaboration with Zumtobel to create a series of lighting ladders which have been inserted into the exposed concrete slab. These direct light onto the concrete, helping to accentuate the aesthetic of the original material, bringing colour – via fabric panel inserts – into the space and improving acoustics.

As Kincaid says, 'this is a project with a strong sense of identity and architectural importance. Our concept seeks to retain the spirit of the original design by taking cues from the order and proportions of the existing building, while maximising usage of the ground-floor space and keeping interior architecture interventions to a minimum. The result is a space with a real warmth and energy about it.'

This project encapsulates the practice's approach to curating ways of living and applies this to the arrival experience within the building. It highlights how it is possible to draw on experience from numerous sectors, blurring the boundaries between work, leisure and design typology to create strong, characterful places.

Place   200 Gray's Inn Road, London

'Our concept seeks to retain the spirit of the original design by taking cues from the order and proportions of the existing building, while maximising usage of the ground-floor space.'
– Simon Kincaid

The hinterland around London's Waterloo Station is one of London's most complex areas. It is a meeting place for major rail and road routes, a destination for thousands of commuters and tourists and a location for diverse buildings within a streetscape that is always characterful, but occasionally challenging. Working within this context, Conran and Partners was asked by Lambeth Council – via an open competition – to design a mixed-use building in Lower Marsh which would offer new retail and workspaces, whilst creating a particular sense of place. The colourful nature of immediately adjacent areas such as The Vaults Theatre and Leake Street tunnel – characterised by its street art – contributes to the sense of Lower Marsh as a distinctive and idiosyncratic place, set apart from the more commercial adjoining areas of Waterloo and the South Bank.

'Lower Marsh has long supported a vibrant, independent, lively community', says Victoria Whenray. 'We sought to develop a scheme which complemented the diverse streetscape and its market, while recognising the potential to create a new area of public space that carries through to the archways under the station.' Waterloo has little in the way of green or open space and so the practice felt it was important to create a new public area, Granby Square, which is visible and readily accessible from Lower Marsh and occupies the borderland between street and station.

The proposal incorporates retail – including a restaurant or café – on the ground floor and office space across the four levels above. Office space is of a scale that will be appropriate for co-working, accommodating small businesses which will benefit from the site's close proximity to Waterloo Station.

Brick cladding is used to create a warm, familiar and contemporary presence on the streetscape of Lower Marsh itself. To the rear, the building steps down, offering a number of roof terraces overlooking the courtyard. A brick colonnade is formed along the courtyard's north side. A blend of hardscaping, seating and planting defines the new area of open, public space which – in turn – connects with Lower Marsh via a newly created arcade and a historic lane running alongside the original Waterloo arches.

'Our approach to the materiality and detailing of the external envelope is influenced by the materials, colours and textures of the surrounding buildings and structures', says Whenray. 'We wanted to explore the opportunity to create spaces between the buildings which didn't exist previously, helping to play a wider role of binding together the neighbourhood they serve.'

Conran and Partners has adopted an approach which is contextual in terms of the hierarchy and form of the building. As a result, the colourful design seeks to respond as much to the granular nature of the back of the development as to the streetscape of Lower Marsh, drawing upon the established rhythms and grains of the building types. 'The terraced nature of the building creates relief to the context and an opportunity for greening and outdoor occupation', says Whenray. 'At the same time generous, framed glazed openings generate light and airy internal spaces whilst providing a connection with the outside world – the activity within is framed and becomes part of the backdrop to the new plaza.'

The local authority wanted to create an exemplar design as a way of demonstrating to developers what can be done to make a positive contribution to the architecture of the area as well as to the wider community. There is a strong visual connectivity between Lower Marsh and Granby Place and passers-by are enticed into the space by glimpses of the courtyard and trees from the street. This scheme is about responding to the existing environment by providing a new, attractive and engaging urban cloister where interaction between people can flourish.

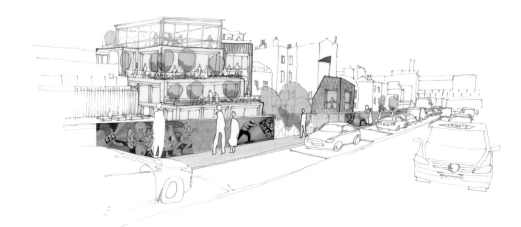

'Lower Marsh has long supported a vibrant, independent, lively community. We sought to develop a scheme which complemented the diverse streetscape and its market.'
– Victoria Whenray

Conran and Partners' work is split equally across architecture and interior design. Many projects engage both disciplines, contributing to a holistic design approach. Over the years, Conran and Partners has demonstrated an intuitive understanding of the inherent connections between the residential, commercial and hospitality sectors, and the way in which the digital world has facilitated far more mobile ways of living, working and playing. By recognising that people's lives overlap and intersect far more than ever before, the practice has developed a forensic approach of looking afresh at every element of design and how it can most effectively respond to a changing world.

Conran and Partners continues to be recognised internationally for its high-profile hotel and restaurant design projects, and its portfolio continues to grow across this sector. These projects allow the practice to play to its strengths – creating distinctive, often dramatic, spaces and buildings. Many of the ideas driving projects of this type are now informing other areas of the practice's work, with the close relationship between hotel and residential projects as a key example. A similar crossover is increasingly evident in the workplace sector, where employees and employers alike seek more relaxed, non-corporate lifestyle solutions.

Residential opportunities – from single buildings to large-scale regeneration projects – will continue to be a key focus for Conran and Partners in the UK and internationally. While the practice gains substantial publicity for its high-end apartment developments it continues to design significant social and mixed-tenure programmes. Regardless of the price-point of the project, the practice's priority consistently focuses on the end users' needs and experiences, while aiming to create a sense of place that is both authentic and context-specific.

Conran and Partners' growth has been organic and is balanced by an ambition to maintain a creative studio environment. The partners continue to engage personally with all projects and clients, whatever the project's size or complexity, with individual team members from across the world contributing their unique experiences to the practice's design thinking.

The opening of a permanent studio in Hong Kong supports and builds on opportunities across Asia-Pacific and taps into an exciting new talent pool. Nonetheless, close collaboration between the studios continues internationally, with projects led directly by the partners across the practice to ensure that the work remains true and consistent wherever it is being undertaken.

Conran and Partners is driven by a shared, central narrative, one that is shaped by – and responds to – changing global design perspectives. Most of all, the partners are committed to building on the practice's legacy, staying true to the belief that good design is fundamental to improving the quality of people's lives and should be made available to as many as possible.

< The Cultural Living Room concept, Seoul

Acknowledgements

We would like to thank Lund Humphries for inviting us to produce this book which has given us a rare opportunity to take a step back and reflect on our work and presentation.

Further thanks go to our author Dominic Bradbury; Paul Stelmaszczyk and Robert Torday of Belford Communications for their invaluable editorial contribution; Zoë Bather for her simple and elegant design; and Charlotte Smale who has kept a steady watch over the book's creation.

Of course, we would not have been able to realise this piece of work without our forward-thinking clients, many of whom we have worked with on multiple projects over the years. And, most importantly, it is our creative, international team whose combined expertise has helped to deliver the projects of which we are most proud.

We are, by nature, a collaborative practice in a collaborative industry so we would also like to extend our thanks to the wider teams involved in our projects who contribute creatively to the realisation of so many of the ideas which are showcased in this book.

Tim Bowder-Ridger, Principal, Conran and Partners

About the author

Writer and journalist Dominic Bradbury has written over 30 books on design, architecture and interiors, including *Rabih Hage: Quiet Architecture* (Lund Humphries, 2018), *Richard Seifert: British Brutalist Architect* (Lund Humphries, 2020) and the best-selling *Mid-Century Modern Complete* (2014). Bradbury also works for many leading newspapers and magazines around the world, including *The Financial Times/How To Spend It*, *The Times*, the *Daily Telegraph*, *World of Interiors*, *House & Garden*, *Vogue Living*, and many international editions of *Architectural Digest* and *Elle Decoration*.

Image credits:
Anna Stathaki
Dais Contemporary
Double Decker
Edmund Sumner
Emanuelis Stasaitis
F10
Grain and Meyer Homes
Guy Montagu-Pollock
James Burns
Jean Cazals
Jeremy Sutton-Hibbert
John Maltby
Kit Oates
Kirk Truman
Knight Dragon
Koji Okumura, Forward Stroke Inc
Luke Hayes
LUMA 3D Interactive Ltd
Luxigon
Marcus Peel
Mark Luscombe Whyte
Matthias Aschauer
Miller Hare
Morley von Sternber
Muzeo
Nacasa & Partners Inc
Nawer Artwork
Patrick Williamson
Paul Raeside, OTTO
Paul Winch-Furness
Ray Phillips
Richard John Seymour
Robin Hayes
Steve White, Calvert Studios
Sutanto Photography
Takuya Watanabe
The Neighbourhood
Toby Mitchell, Birch Represents
Today's Brew
V1
Wolfgang Liebentritt
Woo-Jin Park